Human Rights in Russia

Human Rights in Russia

A DARKER SIDE OF REFORM

JONATHAN WEILER

LYNNE
RIENNER
PUBLISHERS

BOULDER
LONDON

Published in the United States of America in 2004 by
Lynne Rienner Publishers, Inc.
1800 30th Street, Boulder, Colorado 80301
www.rienner.com

and in the United Kingdom by
Lynne Rienner Publishers, Inc.
3 Henrietta Street, Covent Garden, London WC2E 8LU

Library of Congress Cataloging-in-Publication Data
Weiler, Jonathan Daniel, 1965–
    Human rights in Russia : a darker side of reform / Jonathan Weiler.
        p. cm.
    Includes bibliographical references and index.
    ISBN 1-58826-279-0 (hardcover : alk. paper)
    1. Human rights—Russia (Federation)   2. Civil rights—Russia
(Federation)   3. Prisons—Russia (Federation)   4. Russia
(Federation)—Politics and government—1991–   I. Title.
    JC599.R9W45   2004
    323'.0947—dc22
                                                2003025710

British Cataloguing in Publication Data
A Cataloguing in Publication record for this book
is available from the British Library.

Printed and bound in the United States of America

The paper used in this publication meets the requirements
of the American National Standard for Permanence of
Paper for Printed Library Materials Z39.48-1992.

5   4   3   2   1

To the memory of my father,
Lawrence Weiler (1919–1973)

Contents

Acknowledgments

There are more people to thank than I will be able to name here. In Russia, many activists and others gave generously of their time. Special thanks there go to Renfrey Clark, Boris Kagarlitsky, Fred Weir, and two Russian women—Emmanuela and Marina—who generously took me in and provided food and shelter. Special thanks also to Lanny Glinberg for helping me adapt to life in Russia during those first challenging weeks, and to Anne Mavity, Jon Klaverkamp, and Vladimir Shuster for their friendship during my time there.

Barbara Hicks, at UNC Chapel Hill, deserves thanks for her patience and support during the process of completing early work on this project.

At Bowdoin College, I was welcomed by a wonderful group of friends who made my time there personally and professionally worthwhile. I want to thank two in particular: Marc Hetherington, a deep source of professional and personal support and cohost with me of the best darned sports radio show in Brunswick, and Pete Coviello, who has been a wonderful friend and confidant, personally and intellectually. Also, Paul Franco, chair of the Department of Government and Legal Studies during my time at Bowdoin, was a great friend and always in my corner, despite the fact that I am a Yankees fan.

Thanks also to the anonymous reviewers for constructive criticism of my manuscript, and special thanks to Michael McFaul for providing an especially in-depth reading of the manuscript and for his professional generosity.

Thanks to Eric Mlyn for his friendship and willingness to read portions of the manuscript and to Danny Rosen for checking in during difficult times and for, along with Marty Beller, running up my phone bill in October.

On the professional side, I want to thank Sally Glover, Lisa Tulchin,

Richard Purslow, and Lynne Rienner for their help and guidance through various stages of the publication process.

The UNC Department of Political Science provided funding for my first trip to Russia in 1995–1996, for which I am grateful. I also received a travel fellowship from the Tinker Family Fellowship fund, while at Bowdoin, for follow-up research in 2002.

Robert Jenkins, director of the Center for Slavic, Eurasian, and East European Studies at UNC, has provided me with an academic home since my return to Chapel Hill.

Heldref Publications granted permission to reprint here substantial portions of my article, "Human Rights in Post-Soviet Russia," which appeared in the Spring 2002 issue of *Demokratizatsiya*. Thanks also to Ron Ahnen for permission to use a table from his dissertation, "Defending Human Rights Under Democracy: The Case of Minors in Brazil." Also, thanks to Ron for helping me think through some of the issues discussed in Chapter 1.

Among my close friends, I want to especially thank Marty Beller, Michael Wolfson, Gayle Kirshenbaum, and Ira Yankwitt for their love and their willingness to listen to me with patience and intelligence as I talked about this subject. Thanks to Danny Barrish and Steve Eisenbach for being there from the very beginning.

To Anne Menkens, editor extraordinaire: I am grateful for her presence in my life.

Thanks to my mom, Alexandra, and sister, Nina, for all their love and encouragement. I love you both very much.

Finally, I'd like to acknowledge my daughter, Lillian, who has been a constant source of joy in my life.

I

Introduction: Framing the Study

Does democracy promote human rights? If so, does the relationship between democracy and human rights hold throughout the transitional period, when a prior authoritarian regime gives way to some form of democratic governance? And do the benefits of democracy for human rights accrue equally to all citizens, regardless of their social station? Should new and old democracies be analyzed together when we are trying to understand the relationship between democracy and human rights? And what impact does neoliberal economic reform have on the relationship between democracy and human rights? These are the questions that animate this study.

During the Cold War, the answers to these questions seemed clear. In fact, the quest for human rights was synonymous with the quest for democracy, which was coterminus with the fight against communism. This view was shared by those in the West who aggressively opposed the Soviet threat, as well as by dissidents in the East, who recognized in Western (liberal) civilization universal values of justice and equality before the law. With the decision of the East German government to open the Berlin Wall in November 1989, and the subsequent capitulation of all communist governments in the former Soviet bloc, came the collapse of the bipolar world that had stood from the end of World War II. Amid pronouncements of the end of history and the triumph of liberal civilization worldwide, new hope emerged for the promised universal values of human rights, democracy, and prosperity.

The dramatic events in the East followed the already far-advanced process of liberalization and democratization in Southern Europe, Asia, and Latin America. By the beginning of the 1990s, there was virtually universal consensus on the appropriate form of government (democracy) and its attendant form of economic organization (capitalism). With the discrediting of authoritarianism in Asia and the Spanish-speaking world, and the global defeat of communism, a virtuous cycle might now assert itself, to the benefit of all citizens.

To be sure, the rosy optimism of the early 1990s has receded, notably in academic circles.[1] However, if there is increasing recognition of the significant tensions between democracy and globalization (or economic liberalization), there remains virtual silence on the central question of the relationship between democracy and human rights. This is because, when it comes to human rights and democratization, the all-good-things-go-together worldview remains largely undisturbed. And even though scholars might readily admit that transition processes can be messy, partial, and unjust in important ways, no serious debate exists within political science as to whether there is any significant trade-off between the transition from authoritarian rule and the level of human rights enjoyed by citizens.[2] Some scholars, like Fareed Zakaria (1997), have noted the growing prevalence of so-called illiberal democracies, in which political rights, though formally granted, do not ensure protection of basic liberal values or the civil rights of citizens.[3] In general, however, scholars of democratization normally assume human rights protections to be central to any definition of a democracy worth fighting for. They also generally have ignored the issue of human rights in post-Soviet Russia, except perhaps to contend that Russia's lapses in this realm are a result of the Soviet legacy and not linked to the transition process itself.[4]

I challenge this central omission and contend that the transition process is reconfiguring, rather than necessarily improving, the profile of human rights abuses in contemporary Russia and in newly democratizing regimes elsewhere. In fact, I argue that there exists substantial evidence that human rights violations have increased dramatically in Russia since the collapse of the Soviet Union and that this finding mirrors developments in other "new democracies." Although these abuses may have less explicit political motivations than did abuses perpetrated by prior authoritarian regimes, the evidence suggests that human rights violations, as an outgrowth of political processes associated with transitions from authoritarian rule, are a serious problem. The profile of the likely victim of violence has changed (fewer activists; more women and other socially disadvantaged people).[5] However, the changing face of the likely victim of human rights abuses should not be confused with a presumption that these abuses are not taking place or do not have serious implications for our understanding of the process of democratization itself.[6]

Defining Some Key Terms

How "Human Rights" Is Measured

One factor that obscures the trend I describe is that the definition of "human rights" commonly used focuses on explicitly *political* violations of human rights. The Political Terror Scale (PTS), a measure widely used in the human rights literature, counts imprisonment, torture, and murder for politically motivated reasons. It mirrors definitions of democracy prevalent in the literature on democratization, in which political democracy prevails when citizens' free participation in political activities is guaranteed. If political processes have adverse consequences for citizens' rights in realms other than those recognized as clearly political or public, those consequences are not viewed as central to an understanding of the process of democratization itself. For example, leaving aside the war in Chechnya (see Chapter 5), the Russian government does not engage in extensive violence against its citizens for "political" reasons.[7] However, ample evidence shows that certain groups of citizens are disproportionately victims of human rights violations due to the adverse effects of political and economic changes on the social position of these Russians. In other words, although politically motivated violations are comparatively low in contemporary Russia, violations of human rights that result from larger political processes are alarmingly high. Such violations merit serious attention by political scientists.

What, then, counts as a human rights violation? In this study, I use a narrowly defined conception of human rights, namely, *life-integrity violations*.[8] I do not measure Russia's human rights record by reference to its miserable poverty and material suffering in the post-Soviet era, though there would be ample support within the theoretical literature on human rights and among Russian human rights activists to support social and economic measures of human rights violations.[9] Instead, I define "physical violence" as imminent threats to bodily integrity, including beatings, torture, murder, rape, and egregious forms of sexual harassment and study levels of physical violence visited upon specific social groups, as well as immediate threats to mortality due to inescapable social circumstances.

The term "physical violence" refers not only to specifically political acts of violence by the Russian government (or by local governments), which represent a tiny portion of the total level of violence evident in Russia today. It also refers to countless encounters between law enforcement and Russian citizens, in which rights of citizens are repeatedly violated, ranging from false arrests to excessive incarceration, blackmail, physical abuse, and outright violence. Furthermore, as human rights observers have noted for several years, the conditions in Russian prisons are so appalling, and the resulting level of sickness and mortality so egregiously high, that the problem is generally viewed in systemic terms. An outbreak of tuberculosis (TB) in a single prison, no matter how deadly, might not constitute a human rights violation. However, a systemwide pandemic in the face of enormous cutbacks in the procurement of medicine and supplies is a different matter. Thus a policy of maximum incarceration, even for petty crimes, in the context of extreme budgetary restraints whose implications for the physical well-being of prisoners is absolutely predictable and known, in advance, by the state is a policy that violates life-integrity rights.

There may be a distinction between human rights violations specifically targeting individuals, assigning to them the certainty of extreme physical pain or death, and a policy that, by the conditions in which it places its citizens, ensures the extreme physical abuse or death of some nonpredetermined number of individuals. The distinction is between death by direct order versus death by lottery. However, in a lottery there are guaranteed losers, and the distinction, in my view, blurs significantly.

In this sense, I have expanded the definition of the term "life-integrity violations" itself to include violations that arise from the effects of political processes and policies, even if the circumstances are not expressly political. I contend that if political processes have social effects that result in a clear increase in violence directed against socially disadvantaged groups, then we should scrutinize those political processes in terms of those effects. It is also important to view rights of the most fundamental type, including rights to personal inviolability, as not only instrumental for facilitating the coveted political rights associated with polyarchy but also as rights requiring protection in themselves. Jack Donnelly (Ahnen 1999, p. 35, compiled from Donnelly 1989), seeking to refine the usual categories of human rights, offers a sevenfold classification, based on the articles of the Universal Declaration of Human Rights (UDHR):

1. *Personal rights:* rights to life; nationality; recognition before the law; protection against cruel, degrading, or inhumane treatment or punishment; and protection against racial, ethnic, sexual, or religious discrimination (UDHR articles 2–7, 15).
2. *Legal rights:* including access to remedies for violations of basic rights; the presumption of innocence; the guarantee of fair and

impartial public trials; prohibition against ex post facto laws; and protection against arbitrary arrest, detention, or exile and arbitrary interference with one's family, home, or reputation (articles 8–12).
3. *Civil liberties:* especially rights to freedom of thought, conscience, and religion; opinion and expression; movement and residence; and peaceful assembly and association (articles 13, 18–20).
4. *Political rights:* principally the right to take part in government and to periodic and genuine elections with universal and equal suffrage (article 21), plus the political aspects of many civil liberties.
5. *Economic rights:* including principally the rights to work, rest and leisure, and social security (articles 22–25).
6. *Subsistence rights:* particularly the rights to food and a standard of living adequate for the health and well-being of oneself and one's family (article 25).
7. *Social and cultural rights:* rights to education and to participate in the cultural life of the community (articles 26, 27).

Donnelly disaggregates civil rights into three separate components: personal rights, legal rights, and civil liberties. Thus, personal and legal rights are seen as vital, independent categories of human rights, due even to citizens who do not have certain political rights, such as prisoners and minors. Prisoners do forfeit certain rights to political participation and can be legally deprived of liberties such as freedom of movement and residence. However, they retain the most fundamental rights: the right to life and freedom from degrading, inhumane treatment.[10] The concern with personal rights as outlined by Donnelly is central to feminist concerns about human rights as well, because much of the violence and deprivation of life that women suffer is in the private sphere, that is, outside the immediate purview of the state. The focus on the state as the direct culprit in perpetrating human rights violations becomes problematic when feminist critiques of the public-versus-private distinction are taken into account.

If rights of association, conscience, and expression exist only to facilitate the proper functioning of a polyarchy, then it becomes easy to ignore the civil liberties (in which personal rights are subsumed) of those without political rights, whether they are minors, certain categories of criminals, or noncitizens, such as temporary residents and refugees.[11] In the case of women, if their civil liberties, understood in the instrumental sense, are formally intact, then it becomes easy to overlook their personal rights in those spheres in which they regularly participate, though not in explicitly political ways, such as in the home or the workplace. The aggregation of the three components of civil rights (personal rights, legal rights, and civil liberties) into one concept (civil liberties) causes us to miss violations of the most fundamental type. Such aggregation washes out the component parts, and aggregation itself privileges the instrumental value of civil liberties for polyarchy over concerns with human rights more generally.[12] Aggregation also fails to recognize that a weak state, though able to uphold certain kinds of rights (like political rights), may be unable to preserve other rights, including the personal and legal rights fundamental to the concept of human rights.

Socially Vulnerable Groups

The socially vulnerable are those groups of individuals who find themselves in social circumstances from which they may be, for legal or other reasons, incapable of extricating themselves.[13] Prisoners, orphans, and conscripts obviously fall into this category on legal grounds. Women, though not necessarily legally bound to a violent home or a threatening workplace,[14] may be, for economic or other social reasons, incapable of extricating themselves from circumstances in which they are vulnerable to violence. Dark-skinned residents of Moscow, could, in theory, avoid trouble if they never left their apartments. The obvious impossibility of doing so, or of returning to their places of origins, which are often war-torn, qualifies them as socially vulnerable. The salient point here is that the social circumstances of all the groups I describe are characterized by growing violence and threats to mortality.

Economic Reform

A teleology prevails in the word "reform" itself, which leads to a presumption that, because we know that capitalism is good in the long run, reforms that are intended to bring about capitalism must ultimately be good as well. Stephen Shenfield (1998, p. 1) articulates this point well:

> According to an interpretation of the situation in Russia still widely advocated by Western commentators and analysts, Russia is undergoing an admittedly painful but necessary transition to a democratic society and market economy. Transition prejudges the long-term viability of the current mode of functioning of the Russian economy, and

implies that Russia's future shape, the endpoint of the supposed transition is not an unknown to be determined empirically, and ex post facto, but is known in advance, at least in rough outline.

Thus "reform" implies improvement, or change for the better. As Stephen Cohen (1999, p. 42) asks, how can the century's worst industrial depression, the colonialization of the Russian economy, and mass impoverishment be characterized as "reform"? I share Cohen's aversion to the word "reform" in this context; however, I use "reform" throughout this book for the sake of convenience, mindful of how problematic, and even perverse, the term can be in describing many aspects of post-Soviet life in Russia.

Along these lines, a crucial assumption underlying the teleology of democratization is the necessity of economic reform. Prior authoritarian and totalitarian regimes were not only morally abhorrent and murderously repressive; they were economically incompetent as well. For many scholars and other commentators, the goal for Russia and other postauthoritarian regimes is Western-style democracy that is, in turn, undergirded by a free-market economy.[15]

During the third wave of democracy, beginning in the mid-1970s, scholars and leaders concerned themselves primarily with political-constitutional transformations. However, the task of economic restructuring, from Latin America to Africa to Eastern Europe, soon rose to the fore. The general program of fiscal austerity, privatization, and liberalization was usually seen as a necessary concomitant of the broader process of democratization. The relationship between market reforms and democratic consolidation may be uneasy—with growing economic inequality causing mistrust of the democratizing system, for example—but market reforms also produce some of the necessary foundations of a stable democracy, including interest groups and a well-articulated civil society. Dual transitions were necessary in the former Soviet bloc countries in order to break the stranglehold of the Communist Party on the political system and that of the command-based administrative system on the economy. To dismantle the command systems, it was often contended that rapid economic transitions, or "shock therapy," had become the primary goal, even at the expense, in the short term, of certain democratic practices.[16] The advocacy of shock therapy also flowed from an undeniable reality: the Soviet bloc countries were in deep economic crisis. Thus drastic approaches were necessary, if not ideal, according to the prevailing wisdom. Much as democratic elections have become the "only game in town" for more and more states, so too has neoliberal reform become the only conceivable alternative to command economies.[17]

Most influential scholars of democratic transitions identify the following as basic institutional requisites for democracy: regular voting, some form of representative democracy, and legal protections that are wedded to a notion of civil society in which property rights are foundational.[18] Scholars also typically contend that property rights, despite the inequalities generated by free markets, constitute a necessary component of a truly independent civil society (independent, that is, from unwieldy state authority). Furthermore, property rights are the foundation of a system of government based on the rule of law, and the clear consensus is that the rule of law is the linchpin of the "ideal political regime" worldwide (Lowenhardt 1995, p. 26).

I do not mean to condemn capitalism in generic terms. Rather, I contend that capitalism's salutary impact on both economic development and democracy should be viewed as historically specific. I also contend that the kinds of economic models ascendant in various historical periods shape concretely the meaning of capitalism.[19] In the current historical period, neoliberalism is the predominant economic model, predicated on a version of "neoclassical" economics, which holds sway in the International Monetary Fund (IMF), the World Bank, and other important international financial institutions (Rodrik 2002). In turn, this model dictates the range of policies available to reforming (even advanced) economies (Fischer 1996, p. 11). In many ways, the predominance of neoliberalism is more clearly ideological than actual. Many elected leaders of newly democratic countries espouse the general principles of market reform, "responsible" spending, free trade, and integration into world markets. In reality neoliberal reforms, like all ideological blueprints, are implemented to a greater or lesser extent, depending upon historical factors, the balance of political forces, and the interests and receptivity of the population. In ideological terms, however, the logic of support for democratic transitions is ultimately linked to support for market reform, because democratizing countries must invariably reform their economies from their unacceptable pasts. This is so even when reform "perpetuates economic models disproportionately advantaging the rich and powerful" (Karl 1997, p. 17). Such reforms derive from a dismissal of all other current and future possibilities and past realities regarding the politically and economically desirable society (Gleason 1995; Dryzek 1996; Leonard 1997).

Historical Background

An understanding of the relationship between economic reforms and human rights violations must be based on an understanding of the course of economic reforms in Russia since its emergence as an independent state in 1992 and of those facets of reform that can most directly affect human rights violations. Beginning with Mikhail Gorbachev's program of perestroika in the late 1980s, the Soviet and then Russian economies have undergone a profound transformation. The results of this transformation have been much debated, but one undeniable outcome has been the sharp drop in gross domestic product (GDP) of the Russian economy. Estimates of the decline range from about 40 percent to 83 percent between 1991 and 1997 (Shenfield 1998). Peter Reddaway and Dmitri Glinski put the decline at 44 percent from 1992 to 1998. It is true that since the financial crisis of August 1998 Russia has experienced strong economic growth, including growth of 5 percent in 2002.[20] However, average incomes remain lower than they were on the eve of the 1998 crisis (Yavlinsky 2003). Furthermore, over the entire period since Russia became independent, although disagreements exist about the type of production that is being lost,[21] there is a consensus that the economy has suffered a contraction of historic proportions.[22] One consequence has been a dramatic fall in life expectancy for Russian citizens.[23] According to Russian statistics, in 1987 men lived on average to the age of sixty-five. By 1996, that figure had dropped to fifty-eight, an astonishing decline, especially in peacetime. Women have seen their life expectancy drop as well, from seventy-four in 1989 to seventy-one in 1996 (Juviler 1998, p. 161).

As of 2003, life expectancy was fifty-nine for men and seventy-two for women.[24] In sum, Russia's intertwined economic and political transformations have had dire consequences for the life chances of millions of its citizens.

Shock Therapy

President Boris Yeltsin's decision to launch radical economic reform at the beginning of 1992 has been at the center of controversy about the causes of these developments. Scholars have typically referred to this package of reforms as "shock therapy," which has five major components: (1) liberalization of prices and of the ruble itself; (2) macroeconomic stabilization, including significant reductions in government spending and the limitation of the money supply; (3) privatization of state enterprises; (4) abolition of the remaining elements of central planning, including state orders for goods and full employment; and (5) removal of barriers to trade and investment.[25] Two of the central questions about the implementation of shock therapy are whether it went too far or not far enough and whether, in fact, it is fair to characterize Russia's economic reform as shock therapy at all. It is beyond the scope of this study to explore in depth the many facets of this complex debate. David Kotz and Fred Weir's account forcefully contends that Russia (through 1997) had pursued a radical course of reform, particularly in privatization, in fiscal austerity, and in the growth of unemployment following the abandonment of guaranteed employment under Soviet rule.[26] Reddaway and Glinski (2001, p. 235) similarly contend that "under the circumstances, Yeltsin's policies were the closest feasible approximation to Sachs' and the IMF's original intentions, and in this sense, the present perverted form of Russian robber baron 'capitalism' is the unavoidable product of the recipes purveyed by the shock therapists."

Others, notably Anders Aslund and Jeffrey Sachs, have contended that Russia stopped short of a sufficiently vigorous reform, particularly in its expansionary credit policies following the appointment of central banker Viktor Gerashchenko in early 1992. Furthermore, many analysts note that Russian reforms lagged behind other former Soviet bloc countries (notably Poland) by not promoting and developing small businesses and in retaining a bizarre and punitive tax code (Goldman 2003).

One facet of Russian economic reform that did proceed rapidly was privatization. As Marshall Goldman points out, by the end of 1996 Russia had privatized 80 percent of its state sector, a much more rapid rate than that achieved by Poland and China, regarded as two of the most successful examples of capitalist reform (1996, p. 317). In fact, one supporter of shock therapy (Blasi, Kroumova, and Kruse 1997), contends that the pace of Russia's privatization process was unprecedented in world history. The rapid pace of privatization has engendered an extraordinary degree of corruption, particularly in the notorious loans-for-shares scheme that transferred billions of dollars in state resources into private hands through the process of bank-sponsored auctions.[27] These auctions resulted in rampant "insiderism," whereby banks with strong connections to government "won" auctions for large stakes in Russia's nickel deposits, natural gas reserves, telecommunications infrastructure, and other lucrative resources (Hoffman 2002; Goldman 2003). This aspect of privatization was supposed to generate substantial revenue for the government, but the auctions were rigged such that the bank sponsoring the auction invariably won after excluding other potential bidders and then paying a price well below market value.

Russia did privatize very quickly. However, as Goldman has pointed out, the manner in which privatization was carried out has had negative consequences for state resources and capacity. This is so because the corruption resulting from privatization deepened the presence of "dysfunctional institutions" in Russia and because the state got so little value for its assets (Goldman 2003).[28] In turn, these negative consequences have had an adverse impact on the government's ability to enforce its laws and to meet its fundamental legal obligations as resources declined and the rule of law was further undermined. Hoffman (2002, p. 236) notes that in weak states, amid widespread corruption, "selective prosecution" becomes the norm and "the rulers can decide arbitrarily who will be caught and punished." Although Hoffman is referring to elite-level politics and the favoritism paid to insider businessmen, the point holds for the groups of individuals who are the focus of this study.

Another relevant feature of shock therapy is fiscal austerity. One axiom of current economic wisdom is that governments must reduce their role in the economy as much as possible (Friedman 1999; Stiglitz 1999). In order to restrain inflation and create an investment climate suitable for domestic and foreign capital, governments must curtail spending relative to the size of the economy. Kotz and Weir (1997, p. 170) point out that in 1991 government spending as a percentage of GDP for the Russian Federation was about 48 percent. By 1995, that figure had dropped to 27 percent.[29] In fact, the depth of austerity is even more striking when we consider that Russia's GDP has declined so precipitously: in absolute terms, government spending is dramatically lower than it was in the early 1990s. This austerity has a direct impact on the capacity of state institutions to enforce laws. For example, the sharp reduction in government spending on the military and on prisons (especially on basic necessities such as medicine and new infrastructure) directly imperils the health of individuals within those institutions, in violation of Russia's clear constitutional and international commitments to preserve the basic means of life. The fact that citizens are in these institutions not by choice, but rather by law, raises serious human rights concerns when those institutions become incapable of protecting individual well-being at such a fundamental level.

Furthermore, unemployment has grown dramatically since 1992. Joblessness peaked in June 1999 at 14 percent and was at just more than 9 percent at the end of 2002.[30] It is true, of course, that many Russians work off the books, which leads some observers to suggest that the official data overstate actual unemployment. Others note that, given persistent crises in wage arrears as well as the widespread practice of providing in-kind payments as a substitute for wages, unemployment figures may understate the true extent of the problem (Desai and Idson 2000; Javeline 2003). The implications of all this for poverty and hunger are clear enough. However, the implications for human rights are also significant, though complex. For example, the increasing tumult in Russia's labor market and the attendant decline in the number of jobs that pay a livable wage have forced many women into the sex trade, where they become more vulnerable to violations of physical integrity. Additionally, chronic nonpayment of wages to Russia's conscripts and its prison guards almost certainly exacerbates the propensity to violence of those individuals, given the other stresses evident within the institutions in which they work. Finally, growing levels of poverty have direct consequences for levels of crime and violence in society, which in turn jeopardize socially vulnerable individuals and subject more individuals to socially vulnerable circumstances, as is evident in Russia's burgeoning prison system.

In conclusion, it is clear that some elements of Russia's proposed shock therapy were more readily implemented than others. All elements of the reform were shot through with corruption and a degree of skullduggery that surely compromised the original goals of at least the more idealistic reformers. Furthermore, it is important to note the degree to which the Soviet legacy crippled efforts at a more orderly and far-reaching reform process. Among the important legacies are the Soviet Union's decaying physical plant, the traumas associated with the breakup of the empire, and "spontaneous privatization," whereby the "red directors" were pilfering Soviet assets before the onset of reform (Goldman 2003). These legacies have led Stephen Kotkin to contend that there was no neoliberal reform in Russia, nor could there have been, given the broken institutions responsible for overseeing the economic transformation.[31] However, certain key features of post-Soviet Russia—including rapid privatization, with its concomitant impact on state resources; the social chaos that resulted from the reform process, including the dramatic increase in crime; the surge in unemployment; and the shredding of the social safety net—are all attributable, in significant measure, to the 1990s reforms regardless of whether those were the intentions of the people directing the reforms. Defenders of Anatoly Chubais, Yegor Gaidar, and other leading architects of reform note the necessity of compromising with the "red directors" during the initial wave of privatization. Goldman notes, however, that the young reformers all believed strongly in Coase's theorem, whereby privatization, regardless of corruption, was to be pursued at all costs. The underlying premise of the theorem is that once property is in private hands then market forces will push out bad managers in favor of good ones. In other words, the reformers determined that privatization was a top priority, regardless of its short- to medium-term social effects, because in the long run property relations would be sorted out optimally. Regardless of the messiness of real-world implementation, neoliberal ideology, as promulgated in Russia, was clear-eyed about the consequences and was committed to the priorities.[32]

It is true that the Russian version of neoliberalism was constrained and compromised in critical ways. However, the commitment to privatization, the deprioritization of social protection, and the advocacy of property relations favorable to a relative handful of people, with the attendant rise in inequality, were realized and impacted socially vulnerable individuals.[33] The case studies delineate more precisely the relationships between aspects of economic reform, political decentralization, and human rights violations.

Decentralization

One of the primary goals of reform under Gorbachev was to break the monopoly of power held by the Communist Party of the Soviet Union (CPSU) over all facets of life. Soviet reformers viewed overcentralization of political and administrative authority as undemocratic and as a major impediment to efficient decisionmaking. Gorbachev's early reform efforts were aimed at restructuring enterprises, so that economic decisionmaking became the task of enterprise directors, not state planners. His later efforts at political restructuring had a parallel goal: to expand and decentralize input into decisionmaking structures, both in the service of democratic reform and to restrain the CPSU monopoly.[34] In addition to political and economic decentralization, centrifugal pressures from the constituent Soviet republics began to exert a strong influence on Soviet politics. Despite Gorbachev's resistance to rising nationalism, demands for autonomy and then independence intensified in 1990 and 1991 (Brown 1996; DeBardeleben 1997). Yeltsin, as leader of the Russian Federation, had every interest in encouraging nationalism as well as in attacking the CPSU's hold on power; this remained a major source of Gorbachev's authority until the party's demise following the failed coup of August 1991.

In the period 1987–1991, therefore, the major reform efforts in the Soviet Union aimed at curtailing a monstrous, centralized bureaucracy that was deemed unaccountable to popular pressures. Such efforts meshed with the broader sentiment that the major threat to freedom comes from an overbearing state (Holmes 1997). After Russia became an independent state at the beginning of 1992, it faced its own centrifugal pressures, notably from the ethnic republics of Chechnya and Tatarstan. By 1994 the central government had established or was negotiating power-sharing arrangements with eighty-eight of the eighty-nine constituent regions that make up the Russian Federation, in what is often termed *asymmetrical federalism* (McFaul 2001, p. 314). The lone holdout, of course, was Chechnya (Graham 1995). In theory, decentralizing trends are associated with greater responsiveness to the needs of people in particular localities; however, this may not always be the case. Michael McFaul (2001, p. 331) contends that "decentralization and the rising power of regional leaders constitute the most important check on authoritarian rule emanating from Moscow"; however, he also acknowledges that the center's ability to implement national policies through regional governments has weakened substantially since the early 1990s and notes that "the weakness of the center also has allowed local dictatorships to consolidate."[35] And despite President Vladimir Putin's efforts to consolidate the eighty-nine regions of the Russian Federation into seven superregions as part of his effort to strengthen the central apparatus, evidence suggests that the underlying fragmentation that he inherited has not changed materially (Goorha 2001; Holmes 2001).

In general, "federalism" need not be synonymous with "decentralization." For example, Putin's consolidation of the regions into seven superregions is not in itself an attempt to eliminate federalism. However, I view asymmetrical federalism as one form of decentralization to the extent that regional political authority becomes unaccountable to central authorities. I also examine administrative, or institutional, decentralization, in which oversight of state institutions, such as prisons and the military, appears to be diminishing, leaving greater discretion to lower-level state agents. The impetus for reform in the late Soviet period came from the belief that the centralized organs of power were an imminent and constant threat to freedom. Restraints on those organs and then their dissolution became the central concerns of democratic and capitalist reformers in Russia.

However, instead of the clear hierarchy of Soviet authority, in which subordinate institutions were accountable to central structures, institutions in Russia today often ignore federal laws. Instead, bureaucratic politics is characterized by interinstitutional competition for a diminishing pool of resources, and the central leadership appears unwilling or incapable of compelling bureaucracies to uphold the law.[36] When institutions become unaccountable to law or to nominally superordinate authorities, they become what I call microtyrannies. Families can also degenerate into microtyrannies when the law will not intercede to prevent illegal and life-threatening behavior. Whether in geographical or institutional terms, a pervasive lack of accountability to the law, engendered by declining state capacity on the material and moral levels, can be dangerous to socially vulnerable individuals, or those who especially need the state to protect fundamental rights.

I do not propose a unilinear relationship between the process of decentralization and the attendant decline in horizontal accountability, on the one hand, and the level of human rights abuses on the other. Rather, decentralization, both geographical and institutional, interacts in complex ways with other patterns of liberalization, particularly economic reforms, to undermine the human rights of large groups of Russian citizens. The diminishing accountability of all levels of government to constitutional norms and other loci of authority makes post-Soviet Russia, in some surprising ways, less responsive to citizens' needs than in Soviet times and, I would add, less able or willing to protect the personal inviolability of large categories of citizens.

Sources of Data

This is a qualitative study. Because the Russian government does not compile systematic data on violent deaths in prison or on abuse of women in the home, I have had to cull my data from a variety of non-governmental sources. Amnesty International (AI), Human Rights Watch (HRW), and the U.S. State Department issue annual reports that, while not compiling uniform measures of human rights violations, provide detailed anecdotal accounts of the efforts being made by countries to comply with prevailing norms of human rights; they also document, where possible, evidence of systematic violations of rights and well-publicized cases of individual violations. In the past, the two most noted sources for human rights, AI and the State Department, have diverged widely in their assessments of many countries. Critics of each source claimed that ideological influence bore heavily on the findings presented. These differences have been less acute since the late 1980s, and it is now fair to view the sources as complementary and overlapping rather than contradictory.

In addition to the country reports, both AI and HRW produce periodic reports on issues of specific concern, such as AI's 1997 study of prison conditions in Russia. The Russian government, between 1993 and 1996, sustained a human rights task force, led by the famous former dissident Sergei Kovalev, which compiled reports that combined anecdotal accounts with available data similar to the AI and State Department country reports, though in greater detail.[37] A commission under the direction of Oleg Mironov has also provided detailed reports of human rights violations in Russia.[38] Moscow Helsinki Group (MHG) has monitors in all eighty-nine regions of the federation and now compiles its own detailed annual report on human rights.

In addition to these monitoring instruments, I utilize press accounts, as well as personal interviews conducted with human rights activists during ten months of research in Russia from September 1995 to July 1996 and during a two-week trip to Moscow in January 2002. Where possible, I have made use of scholarly accounts. However, excluding abuses associated with the two wars in Chechnya, there has been scant attention in the scholarly literature to the issues described in this book. There has been increasing attention paid to President Putin's campaign against the independent media in Russia and to the harassment of human rights and other activists. These are important human rights violations, and Sarah Mendelson, and James Goldgeier and Michael McFaul (2003), among others, have brought attention to these issues.[39] However, regarding the kinds of violations discussed in this study, there remains little scholarly work. Furthermore, the issues raised have been characteristic of post-Soviet Russia and have persisted into the Putin regime and are not specifically a product of his rule.

The lack of systematic and uniformly coded data represents an inescapable weakness in any effort to depict accurately the state of human rights in Russia. However, I contend that the weight of the available evidence suggests negative change over time with respect to human rights violations. And I also suggest that such changes are themselves a product of changes associated with reform, both political and economic, since Russia became independent in 1992.

Why Russia?

Many scholars contend that Russia is unique and therefore a poor focus for a comparative research agenda. Its long history of autocracy, followed by its unique experience with Stalinism and the durability of communism, make Russia incomparable. Scholars and observers of Russia attribute (too easily, in my view) the difficulties to internal cultural or character factors, and I think it is profoundly misleading to do so. Thus, although this study is intended as an in-depth analysis of human rights violations in Russia, the trends I describe are evident in many parts of the world (see Chapter 6). Furthermore, in considering how Russia might address some of these problems, it is important not to focus solely on factors that are internal to Russian culture and politics, though historical legacies undeniably bear the trends I describe. It is impossible, in my view, to ignore the global context.

Moreover, no scholar of Russia questions seriously whether human rights are better protected now than they were in Soviet times, because the Soviet Union was the exemplar of the rights-denying regime. It denied human rights to all citizens; its repression was total. Scholars do criticize many aspects of the transitional process, but when it comes to human rights Russia is still evaluated with reference to the bipolar ideal-types that were prevalent during the Cold War. The totalitarian past was unacceptably bad; the endpoint to which Russia presumably aspires—some form of democracy—is fundamentally good. Therefore, when it comes to human rights, if any country should unambiguously benefit from the demise of its prior authoritarian regime, it is Russia. The fact that it isn't is noteworthy and seems to contradict what we assume about state power and its connection with human rights abuses.

Weak States and Human Rights Violations

Given the current state-centric structure of the international system, human rights regimes rely on member states to enforce internationally recognized rights. As an analytical matter, it is important to understand that abusive or predatory states, though still in existence, may no longer provide an adequate model or guide to the mechanisms whereby human rights are most regularly violated. Indeed, our very conception of the state as the main threat to human rights has a historical pedigree, one that influences our understanding of the sources of human rights violations. The fact that the strong state was a force destructive of human rights in the past does not necessarily mean that a weak state will result in better quality of life and freedom from human rights abuses.

Historically, natural rights that individuals held inalienably were rights that they held against the absolutist states of the time. The modern concept of a social contract was one in which the state demanded increasing compliance from citizens in exchange for which citizens (originally, property-holding men) demanded more rights as a "shield" against the ambitious intrusion of authority (Madsen 1996, p. 11). The twentieth-century experience of modern, terroristic regimes that brutalized populations only reinforced the belief that the state represents the greatest threat. However, even if this has been the case, it does not automatically follow that states have always posed, or will continue to pose, the primary challenge.

The abuses we commonly associate with the Soviet Union—political repression in the most widely accepted sense—derived from an overly intrusive state that used its overwhelming resources to interfere in virtually every sphere of life. However, the current problem in Russia stems from a state that is too weak to sustain an adequate judicial apparatus, reasonably functioning law enforcement, and prisons that meet minimal standards of humanity. State agents continue to abuse power in egregious and systematic ways. However, the massive violations of the most fundamental rights of criminals and criminal suspects, as well as other socially vulnerable groups, stem as much from the inadequacy of the state as from its repressive qualities. In fact, the brutality of the Russian state today is itself a product, in large measure, of the basic incapacity of the state to function. In other words, brutality and corruption among the police are not the result of a deliberate state policy to undermine the rights of citizens through a terroristic internal security apparatus. Rather, brutal practices result from the fact that the state lacks the capacity to check its own bureaucracies, or to fund them adequately to do the jobs that the law stipulates.[40] The state's formal commitments, as evinced by the constitution of the Russian Federation and the legal reforms undertaken since its formation, are to uphold individual human rights (something that the Soviet state expressly denied in important respects). However, the practices of state agents trend in a different direction.

One form of abuse—that visited upon prisoners and potential victims of police abuse—arguably derives from state abuses of power that liberal rights seek to prevent. A second form of abuse derives from the blind spots inherent in liberalism itself, namely, the insistence on the public/private distinction that is at the heart of liberal theory. Although the Soviet regime became in many respects less intrusive in personal life after Joseph Stalin, it continued to insist on the supremacy of its own prerogatives over any right to privacy as understood in the West. One unintended consequence was that the Soviet state was more likely to intervene in domestic abuse, for its own purposes, than in Russia today. Although females in Russia, like males, are subject to the rapacious forces of unchecked and corrupt police and indifferent or incapacitated state agencies, they are also left to fend for themselves in spheres in which the state no longer sees itself as legitimately active—namely, the home and the workplace. In other words, the state's "liberal" commitments, absent other protections, put women in a dangerous position given the growing violence of daily life. The state's incapacity thus potentially jeopardizes life for all citizens. The collapse of public power is indiscriminate; however, the effects of the substitution of private power for state power discriminates in particular ways. The victims of abuse that flows from state incapacity are not entirely random. Rather, they are often those who are already socially vulnerable—easy prey for unaccountable microtyrannies.

Outline of the Study

Chapters 2 and 3 present case studies in which I examine the context for, and trends in, life-integrity violations of prisoners (Chapter 2) and women (Chapter 3). Chapter 2 explores the deteriorating conditions in Russian prisons, which, I argue, result largely from the difficult fiscal conditions confronting the Russian state under economic liberalization and of law enforcement policies leading to overcrowding. The central state (as well as local authorities) have responded to an explosion in lawlessness by resorting to draconian methods of fighting crime, including the extreme use of incarceration, even for individuals suspected of petty offenses. The burgeoning prisons lack the resources necessary to treat prisoners in a manner consistent with Russia's laws or international obligations. The result is that more individuals are going to jail for minor transgressions; the level of mortality of those in the system, according to the available evidence, is rising.

In Chapter 3, I contend that even though ordinary crime does not represent a human rights violation, systematic differences in the enforcement of existing laws do represent a human rights issue. In this instance, the level of violence against women in post-Soviet Russia rises to the level of a human rights problem. Violence, including the murder of women in the home, is widespread in post-Soviet Russia, and the evidence overwhelmingly suggests that law enforcement officials simply refuse to pursue domestic violence cases seriously. The murder of women in the home, and their rape or abuse in the workplace, are physical-integrity violations that rise to the level of human rights violations because the state's gross negligence in this matter virtually ensures, given other factors, high levels of violence against women. When a state *perpetrates* violence, it is a presumptively political, or "public," act. When a state *countenances* violence, it is viewed differently, the problem that scholarship is most likely to overlook. Most scholars' conception of human rights flows ineluctably from a constrained conception of what is properly "political." If an outcome is politically motivated, the scholarship recognizes this as a "violation." If an outcome is induced by a sociopolitical context, this is viewed as an unfortunate side effect of "reform" (if it is recognized at all). Extending the argument about abuses of power in microtyrannies from Chapter 2, I contend that this privatization of power has particularly negative consequences for women. The growth of alcoholism and poverty and the liberalization of travel restrictions all contribute to growing violence against women in this context.

In Chapter 4, I outline human rights violations against three other social groups. These include children, military conscripts, and dark-skinned residents of Moscow, including immigrants from the southern regions of the former Soviet Union. Some might contend that prisoners, because of their status as convicted (or suspected) criminals, should not be viewed as having rights in the sense that ordinary citizens do. Others might contend that violence in the home, though a serious concern on humanitarian grounds, is not a human rights violation worthy of systemic attention in the way that public violations are. Although I challenge these arguments in Chapters 2 and 3, I use Chapter 4 to show that problems associated with Russia's regime change have negative consequences for human rights for individuals clearly located in public spaces. Further, these individuals find themselves in public spaces not because of any criminal wrongdoing but because of circumstances beyond their control.

The breakdown of the system of social protection that prevailed under Soviet rule has led to growing numbers of abused and abandoned children, an increasing number of whose parents are simply giving up responsibility for their care. Once abandoned, many children end up in the state orphanage system, where the effects of fiscal austerity and over-burdened facilities have engendered widespread abuse amid appalling conditions. Similarly, the near-total collapse of Russian military resources has led to catastrophic health problems among conscripts, including a substantial increase in mortality in the military. High levels of violence that result from brutal hazing rituals and starvation-level rations characterize life for many young soldiers.

There is extensive documentation of the persecution and arbitrary arrest of dark-skinned migrants from the Southern Caucasus, especially by Moscow police. Moscow's relatively strong economy has made it a haven for Russians. As a result, a residence permit is a cherished resource for those looking to improve their life chances or to escape ongoing strife along the southern borders. Moscow authorities have responded to this influx of refugees by targeting dark-skinned individuals for harassment, arrest, and expulsion from the city limits. The desire of the authorities to maintain Moscow as an oasis in the midst of economic upheaval partly motivates this harassment, as does the use of dark-skinned residents as scapegoats for Moscow's high crime rate. The use of violence during "document checks" and the arbitrary arrests of dark-skinned residents are commonplace.

In Chapter 5, I discuss the two wars in Chechnya. The origins of the first war (1994–1996), and the political context within which it was fought, differed from those of the current conflict, which began in 1999. However, from the standpoint of human rights, the two wars are strikingly similar. As a singular event, war is obviously distinct from the cases that make up the heart of this study. However, any discussion of human rights in post-Soviet Russia must confront Russian incursions into Chechnya. In both instances, the extraordinary brutality, the number of casualties, and the fact that the great majority of deaths were noncombatants make it an appropriate subject for discussion in a study of human rights in Russia. In fact, it is arguable that Russia's fragmenting state and declining capacity contributed to both disastrous forays into Chechnya. Following Anatole Lieven's (1998a) excellent account, I develop this argument in Chapter 5. Atrocities committed by Chechen forces are also an undeniable reality of the conflict, more so in the second war than in the first, according to available information.

In the Conclusion (Chapter 6), I put Russia's human rights record in comparative perspective. I contend that the growing phenomenon of socially driven abuses of life integrity is a phenomenon widely observable in new democracies throughout the world. This fact necessitates explanations suggesting that there are global or structural processes influencing levels of life-integrity violations. In Brazil, for example, the end of authoritarian rule and the emergence of political democracy have been accompanied by an extraordinary increase in assassinations of street children. Overwhelmingly, the victims are poor and are concentrated in Brazilian *favelas*, or slums, in which both police and private security forces act capriciously. Recent reports by HRW on prison conditions in Brazil and a major United Nations (UN) study about prison conditions in Eastern Europe all suggest similar patterns: rising crime and growing police impunity in the context of severe fiscal austerity and an ineffective juridical apparatus. I outline factors that may be driving these outcomes cross-nationally.

I do not offer a blanket condemnation of all aspects of Russian life associated with the regime change away from single-party rule. For example, however problematic Russian elections have been, they obviously represent a dramatic step forward for Russians' ability to influence the composition of elite decisionmakers. Similarly, despite disturbing developments under Putin, there has emerged in Russia a raucous and often highly critical independent press. Additionally, hundreds of thousands of independent organizations have emerged to organize interests and to press the government for redress of grievances, including thousands devoted to human rights alone.[41] As a result, many scholars of Russia, in however qualified terms, believe that some form of democracy has emerged there.[42] I do not dispute that broad characterization; nor do I contend that democracy itself is responsible for the abuses described in this book. I do contend that myriad social problems, including widespread inequality, poverty, and violence, have attended regime change globally since the end of the Cold War and that these problems are, in part, consequences of the transition from authoritarian rule. In turn, the unsettled and unsettling social context to which citizens have struggled to adapt in these regimes has preyed disproportionately on specific, socially vulnerable groups.

It is not a given that human rights would improve under democratization; nor are abuses to be treated as extreme cases, that is, exceptions to the expected teleology of democratic change. Scholars too often do take this teleology for granted.[43] A poor human rights record, even one that is worse than under a prior regime, is not necessarily a temporary phenomenon or the product of an unconsolidated regime. It is a reality that scholarship on democracy must confront more seriously as a legacy of a stratifying global economy. If formal democracy accompanies a decline in state resources that in turn makes actors—state and private—less accountable to the law, then human rights of the most fundamental kind may be undermined. If so, then the historical relationship between democracy and respect for human rights may require fundamental reconsideration.

Notes

1. Karl points out that critics from both left and right now fear that "global market integration and democracy are more likely to undermine than support one another" (1997, p. 4). Karl locates the growing disillusionment in the false premises of the earlier optimism about the collapse of communism. She characterizes this optimism as an "unabashed love affair with neo-liberal models and western-style democracy" and locates its intellectual origins in the "wholehearted embrace of political modernization and Rustowian economic growth schools of the 1960s." This embrace is predicated on a central fallacy— "the assumption that all good things come together, e.g., that somehow countries undergoing fundamental transitions can do so without painful trade-offs and violence" (p. 7).

2. Two studies that do assess, quantitatively, the relationship between the transition process and human rights are Fein (1995) and Zanger (1998). Both studies show that there are actual increases in human rights violations, as measured by the Political Terror Scale (PTS), discussed below, as countries move from authoritarian to some form of democratic regime, although these findings are more qualified in Zanger's study than in Fein's. These studies and the quantitative literature on human rights are analyzed in detail in Weiler (1999).

3. Michael McFaul (2001), a noted scholar of contemporary Russian politics, suggests that the appellation of "illiberal democracy" may apply to contemporary Russia. However, the fact remains that there is scant discussion of

the possibility that the transition process itself, or the concomitant features of transition, including economic liberalization, or "shock therapy," would undermine seriously citizens' most basic human rights. For example, in his chapter-length discussion of the nature of Russia's illiberal democracy, McFaul outlines serious problems in the realms of party development, rule of law, weakness of federalism, civil society, and the press but does not mention human rights.

4. Exceptions include Mendelson (2002) and Juviler (1998).

5. Oxhorn, writing about what he calls "neo-pluralism" in Latin America, contends that the "overall level of state violence in these countries has generally not declined. Instead, it has undergone a qualitative change, as it is no longer directed against the political opposition, but the poor" (1999, p. 12).

6. Nancy Scheper-Hughes, in writing about the conditions of children in Brazil and South Africa, calls attention to "forms and spaces of hitherto unrecognized, gratuitous and useless social suffering" and notes that "the things that are hardest to perceive are often those which are right before our eyes and therefore simply taken for granted" (1996, p. 889).

7. There have been numerous well-publicized cases in which authorities have persecuted individuals in clear violation of their constitutionally granted political rights. Well-known cases include those of the former navy captain Alexander Nikitin and the journalist Grigory Pasko. Each was hounded legally by the government for several years for having published damning information on the navy's inability to adequately deal with nuclear waste in its Northern Fleet. All information published by Nikitin already existed in public documents, belying the government's claim that he violated laws on official secrets. There are other "political cases," and a growing campaign of harassment against activists under Vladimir Putin, but the numbers simply do not compare to the regular persecution of dissidents under Soviet rule. I do not attempt, in this study, to claim otherwise. Radio Free Europe/Radio Liberty (RFE/RL) *Newsline*, August 3, 2000.

8. The human rights literature uses the term "life-integrity violations" to describe victims of political terror and torture (see, e.g., Fein 1995). Throughout this study, I will use the terms "personal inviolability," "bodily integrity," "physical integrity," and "life-integrity" interchangeably for the sake of style. In all instances, I intend to suggest that such violations seriously, if not mortally, threaten the physical well-being of individuals.

9. For example, Russia's Presidential Commission on Human Rights, chaired by the eminent former dissident Sergei Kovalev until 1996, deemed nonpayment of wages and growing poverty more generally as central human rights concerns, not only on their own terms but also because of the impact of material deprivation on citizens' ability to enjoy other basic rights (Kovalev 1996a). Oleg Mironov, who succeeded Kovalev, has also focused on these issues. There is a voluminous literature on so-called first-, second-, and third-generation rights, which I discuss in some detail (Weiler 1999). Meyer (1998) provides a useful overview of the three generations of human rights.

10. An important exception to the universal right to life is in the case of the application of the death penalty. Most human rights scholars agree, howev-

er, that the death penalty is unacceptable in all cases because of the inviolability of this most basic right. Major monitoring organizations, such as AI and HRW, view any application of the death penalty, regardless of the legal procedures by which it is carried out, as a violation of this most basic right and an unacceptable practice in all circumstances. The Council of Europe, which is the human rights body of European member states, accepted Russia in February 1996 on the condition that Russia abolish the death penalty within three years. Though Russia suspended executions in September 1996, it still has not passed legislation outlawing the use of capital punishment as of early 2004, though it has not carried out an execution since 1996.

11. Along these lines, Mironov, the surprisingly effective human rights ombudsman for Russia, said in January 2000 that "if you want to create a party or hold a picket, you are welcome to do it." But, he added, "possibly it is the only political freedom which is not violated in Russia." Reuters, "Russians Have Political Freedom, but Little Else," January 27, 2000, from *Johnson's Russia List* (*JRL*), January 27, 2000.

12. Referring to the aggregation of political imprisonment with torture and killing in the PTS, McCormick and Mitchell (1997, p. 511) contend that we cannot properly analyze data about human rights, either globally or in individual countries, when we fail to disaggregate the data appropriately.

13. The categories I use in this study mirror those used in the comprehensive report by the Moscow Helsinki Group (2001). The report obtains information from all regions of the Russian Federation. Although the framework was arrived at independently, the report also uses the term "socially vulnerable individuals"; see Weiler (1999, 2002).

14. It is common in contemporary Russia that, even after a couple is divorced, due to economic stress and housing shortages, they may remain in the same apartment. Even if the husband is known to be physically abusive, he often cannot be compelled to leave the apartment (see Chapter 3).

15. Dahl (1998) and Linz and Stepan (1996), among many others, recognize that markets themselves require institutional constraints without which democracy may be imperiled.

16. Przeworski (1991) advocates such an approach while lamenting its likely effects, including what he describes as the passing of the idea of socialism. Haggard and Kaufman (1996) are also associated with this approach.

17. As I discuss below, neoliberal reform comprises varied approaches in practice, though there exists a discernible underlying logic that animates the many faces of neoliberal reform. Furthermore, there is, of course, serious debate about whether and to what degree one can characterize Russia's economic reforms in the 1990s (and up to the present) as neoliberal or in accord with the so-called Washington Consensus.

18. These include Schmitter and Karl (1991), Linz and Stepan (1996), Huntington (1991), and O'Donnell, Schmitter, and Whitehead (1986).

19. Kotz and Weir (1997, p. 166) contend that shock therapy in Russia is "essentially an application of free-market and Monetarist economic theories to the problem of transforming a state socialist into a capitalist system." Friedman (1999) and Stiglitz (1999) both point out that until very recently many Western

observers praised the East Asian capitalist model, which emphasized substantial state involvement in industrial policy, as opposed to the minimalist state approach now ascendant. In other words, there are many critics of neoliberal reform in Russia and elsewhere who criticize a particular conception of reform based upon an ahistorical understanding of the evolution of capitalism rather than capitalism itself. Other examples include Steele (1994) and Lieven (1998b).

20. The 2002 data are reported in Goskomstat's *Current Statistical Survey*, June 30, 2003.

21. Some scholars contend that the decline in GDP is overstated because, among other things, the Soviet economy was characterized by wasteful "value-subtracting" industries, particularly to feed its oversized military-industrial complex; Aslund (1995, 1997, 2001) and Leitzel (1995), among others, make this claim. However, as Shenfield (1998) points out, there was an 81 percent decline in the production of consumer goods between 1991 and 1997. In fact, relative to the Soviet period, consumer production (whose improvement was a primary aim of economic reformers) has lost substantial ground to Russia's extractive industries, especially oil, gas, and metal. In other words, Russia's economy has undergone a process of "primitivization" since 1991 (Shenfield 1998; Yavlinsky 2003). Reddaway and Glinski (2001, p. 249) contend that only a small portion of the contraction of output represented nonproduction of unwanted goods.

22. It should be noted here that the contraction in Russia clearly started before the breakup of the Soviet Union in December 1991. Kotz and Weir (1997, pp. 75–76) show that GDP began to shrink in 1990 and declined by about 12 percent in 1991.

23. The dramatic decrease in life expectancy is due to a number of factors, including increasing malnutrition, decline in health services and attendant epidemics, a growth in alcoholism, the rise in crime, and stress. All of these factors are substantially attributable to various aspects of the reforms (Lieven 1998a).

24. Irina Titova, "Russian Life Expectancy on Downward Trend," *St. Petersburg Times*, January 17, 2003, from *JRL*, January 18, 2003.

25. These are the categories used by Kotz and Weir (1997, pp. 161–163).

26. Anders Aslund (1997, p. 143), onetime economic adviser to the Russian government and widely cited in the West, contends that Russia's main economic difficulties result from "half-baked and inconsistent reform measures," particularly in the realm of financial stabilization. He also contends that, contrary to most analysis, data for budgetary allocations at all levels show that social spending, as a percentage of GDP, has not declined since 1992. Of course, shock therapy began in 1992, and a better baseline year might therefore be 1991. In any event, Aslund acknowledges that, given the decline in GDP, social spending has declined in real terms. Without explanation he then contends that "share of GDP appears to be the relevant measure" (p. 139). McFaul (2001) similarly contends that social spending remains high, though he criticizes the thrust of the spending as not targeted toward people in need but rather as subsidies that reduce housing and other costs for people already relatively

well-situated. An important point here is that social spending is only one facet of government spending and that the overall decline in government spending has specific implications for human rights (see below).

27. See Hoffman (2002) for an in-depth account of loans-for-shares and the principal actors involved in it.

28. Hoffman (2002, p. 315) reports that the sale of a 38 percent stake in Norilsk Nickel in 1995 earned the government U.S.$170.1 million, when its gross revenues for that year alone were more than $3 billion and it earned profits of more than $1 billion.

29. Reddaway and Glinski (2001) report that whereas the government budget deficit was 30 percent of GDP in 1991, it was 4.8 percent of GDP in 1998. A significant weapon in the fight against deficits was impoundment and sequestration of planned expenditures, including the wages of millions of people. Nonpayment of wages has been less of an issue in the past two or three years.

30. Data are from "Stock Market Soars . . . as Unemployment Rises," *RFE/RL Newsline*, June 22, 1999, and from Goskomstat, June 30, 2003.

31. Kotkin (2001, p. 117) contends that "the Soviet collapse continued through the 1990s, and much of what appeared under the guise of reform involved a cannibalization of the Soviet era."

32. Goldman (2003, p. 65) quotes Gaidar as saying that "I would have acted approximately as I did." Chubais famously said about the oligarchs that "they steal and steal" but that loans for shares were still justified because of the eventual demand that the oligarchs would make for good corporate governance and the rule of law (quoted in Lieven 1998b). However, Joel Hellman (1998) has pointed out that the reform process in Russia created a powerful coalition of interests precisely committed to perpetuating the corrupt circumstances under which they came to power. Thus, contrary to the reformers' assertion that the ends would justify the means in the case of privatization, the means may have foreclosed more socially just results.

33. Remington (2002, p. 224) cites World Bank data showing that Russia had, by 1993, become one of the most unequal societies in the world and has remained so.

34. There are too many accounts of Mikhail Gorbachev and his policies to list them all here. Brown (1996) provides perhaps the most compelling analysis.

35. DeBardeleben (1997, p. 169) also specifically points out that "the incapacity of central state organs to make and implement effective policy has produced a de facto transfer of power to the subnational governments" and that a lack of coherence between federal laws and regional laws is a significant obstacle to properly functioning government. In other words, de facto federalism can lead to anarchical relations between the center and the regions, undermining political stability and governmental accountability. Martha Merritt (1997, p. 362) contends that although "events and issues that used to be tightly closed are now wide open . . . this has not led to a feeling of empowerment: rather power seems to trickle away. . . . Devolution of power from central authority has not necessarily made government more rooted in democratic norms or more accessible for the public."

36. Huskey (1996) contends that Yeltsin's political strategy was to encourage such infighting, so that he could act as the ultimate arbiter of various disputes and therefore be the benefactor for powerful interests. The result was "intentional anarchy." From this perspective the state incapacity that DeBardeleben mentions in connection with regions is a by-product of a particular political strategy (Lieven 1998a, p. 290; see Graham 1995 for a similar argument). Holmes (2001) contends that, despite Putin's administrative moves, this remains the case.

37. Kovalev quit in 1996 in disgust over Russia's conduct in Chechnya and a more general disappointment with Russia's human rights record under Boris Yeltsin (Kovalev 1996b). The government still maintains a human rights task force, though staffed at a much lower level of resources than it was under Kovalev's leadership. "Presidential Commission Preparing Program on Human Rights," *RFE/RL Newsline*, January 16, 1998.

38. Mironov initially concerned himself more with economic violations, such as increases in transportation prices and their impact on Russians' freedom of movement, than with a concern for the kinds of violations I describe here. However, he has taken up a full range of issues relevant to my study.

39. In an article in the *Los Angeles Times*, Goldgeier and McFaul (2003) note that Russia now ranks 121 out of 139 countries in a cross-national study of media freedoms. The attack on press freedom in Russia and harassment of activists more generally, in addition to ongoing violations in Chechnya, have led these scholars to contend that "the evidence of an erosion of democracy in Russia is now overwhelming."

40. See Human Rights Watch (1999, "Confessions at Any Cost: Police Torture in Russia") for extensive documentation of the widespread nature of torture under interrogation in Russia. By all accounts, this problem persists unabated (Bivens 2003).

41. According to Mironov (2002), there are more than 1,500 human rights organizations in Russia.

42. Juviler (1998) uses the term "partial" democracy. Sakwa (1994) characterizes Russia as an "incomplete" democracy. McFaul (1997, 2001) has used the terms "consolidated electoral democracy" and "illiberal democracy." Zakaria (2003) has also used the latter term to describe Russia.

43. For example, Jack Donnelly (1999, p. 14), while acknowledging that many newly democratizing countries violate various internationally recognized rights, still insists that the recent "democratic revolutions have undoubtedly benefited human rights," without specifying who benefits, and in what realms. Linz and Stepan (1996, p. 457), in their very thorough and thoughtful account of challenges facing newly democratizing countries, "acknowledge that some countries will consolidate democracy, but will never deepen democracy in the spheres of gender equality, access to critical social services, inclusive citizenship and respect for human rights and freedom of information. *They might, indeed, occasionally violate human rights*" [emphasis added].

2

Prisons: Resource Deprivation and Torturous Conditions

The Gulag represents perhaps the most notorious and sinister feature of Soviet communism.[1] Most devastatingly unmasked by Alexander Solzhenitsyn, the Gulag became symbolic of life in the Soviet Union, where citizens lacked basic individual freedoms and were subjected to harsh justice, virtually without recourse to due process of law or adequate defense.[2] Therefore, from the standpoint of human rights activists, especially those who had spent years in Soviet labor camps during the 1970s and 1980s, the onset of glasnost and then the deeper processes of democratization were universally welcomed. Mikhail Gorbachev's determination to transform the Soviet Union into a *pravovoe gosudarstvo*—a law-based state—was perhaps the most radical and far-reaching of his many reform efforts.

In fact, Russia has undergone a legal revolution in which the laws and statutes of the Russian Federation, including the Russian constitution, obligate the state to abide by an authority higher than its own authority—namely, the law.[3]

In considering Russia's submission in 1995 of its fourth periodic report to the United Nations Human Rights Committee, the committee welcomed the new constitution, "which gives legal recognition to the concept of human rights and freedom to the individual" and recognizes this development as part of the "progress made toward democracy" in the previous five years (Comments, p. 2). At the same time, the committee expressed "regret that, while the report was mainly drafted on the basis of legal measures enacted or under consideration, insufficient information was provided regarding the actual enjoyment of some of the rights guaranteed" (p. 1). Furthermore, the committee voiced concern that "the profound legislative changes taking place within the State party have not been matched by the actual protection of human rights at the implementation level" (p. 3).

In this chapter, I examine the real-life conditions confronting Russian prisoners today. Despite the legal revolution that has taken place on paper, prisoners are subject to barbarous treatment and conditions that clearly violate Russia's constitutional and international commitments. I contend that economic reform has greatly reduced the state's fiscal resources, with a devastating impact for conditions in prisons. Furthermore, the profound social disruption brought about by reforms, including high levels of poverty and unemployment, contributed to an explosion in crime rates. The response of authorities to the crime wave—to incarcerate even petty criminals for long periods— exacerbated the already difficult conditions in the prisons. At the same time, the general chaos in the state administration has reduced oversight of local institutions, including prisons. One consequence of this is a decline in the legal accountability of prison authorities. As a result, extreme methods of brutality and violence are endemic to the system (even excluding the awful physical conditions).

The decline in horizontal accountability has also affected the court system. Judges have continued to hand down harsh sentences, or refuse to release prisoners for whom there is insufficient evidence to convict, in contravention of federal law. Many scholars contend that the extraordinary levels of crime and corruption and the attendant brutal violation of citizens' rights by the police are artifacts of an incompletely reformed KGB apparatus.[4] Many of the leading members of Russia's law enforcement community do express attitudes and advocate policies that are consistent with the most retrograde features of the Soviet-era police state.[5] Furthermore, many leading law enforcement officials in Russia today are holdovers from the Soviet security apparatus (as is, of course, the current president). However, in important respects there has been a change for the worse for Russia's inmates since 1992, when Russia became an independent state and when it first introduced radical economic reforms.[6] This dynamic requires explanations that focus on changes since 1992. For example, although prosecutorial bias is a continental and Soviet holdover, "the crisis in pre-trial detention, with persons charged with conventional offenses awaiting trial for prolonged periods in over-crowded tuberculosis-infested prisons, is largely a post-Soviet product" (Solomon and Fogelsong 2000, p. 142).

In the remainder of this chapter, I outline some major dynamics of law and order under Soviet rule, particularly after Joseph Stalin. Next I discuss the changing face of crime and punishment since 1992, focusing on the dramatic increase in crime and the authorities' response to that development. I look at the period up to 1996, when the most precipitous changes took place in the dynamics of crime and punishment in post-

Soviet Russia. I also note the stabilization of these trends subsequent to 1996. Then I present broad empirical evidence, culled from reports by major advocacy organizations, including AI, HRW, the Moscow Center for Prison Reform (MCPR), and other Russian organizations, detailing the argument that prison conditions and prisoners' life-integrity rights are worsening. I also discuss some of the political changes that have occurred in Russia, including decentralization of the judicial apparatus and the absence of CPSU control over the bureaucracy. Throughout, I highlight how aspects of the transition process help to explain the increase in life-integrity violations among Russians caught in the penal system. Finally, I note that some recent developments, including the promulgation of a new criminal code and recent prison amnesties, have brought about incremental improvements in the prison system. It remains too early to tell whether these developments will ameliorate the larger trends I describe.

Soviet Prisons

Many scholars have pointed out that the lack of reliable statistics complicates any effort to draw a comprehensive picture of the Soviet penal system (Connor 1972; Chalidze 1977; Shelley 1987, 1996; Sergeev 1998). Until 1989, Soviet crime statistics were classified. Additionally, it is likely that the statistics available to Soviet officials were seriously flawed. Walter Connor (1972, p. 2) has noted that Soviet crime statistics, to the extent that they were available, reflected regime concerns and law enforcement priorities more closely than they did criminality itself. This problem persists. What is clear is that following Stalin's death in 1953 and Nikita Khrushchev's consolidation of power, far-reaching changes were made in the Soviet policing apparatus. These changes included the ending of the terror; greater local involvement in policing; professionalization of the regular police; and increased observance of legal norms (Shelley 1996, p. 38). Khrushchev condemned secret trials, trials in absentia, and the notion of collective responsibility and military jurisdiction over civilians, the last of which was abolished in the mid-1950s (Los 1988, p. 16). It should be clear that Khrushchev's pronouncements did not mean a cessation of such practices. Stalin's death and the rise of "socialist legality" did, however, bring an end to the terror that pervaded Soviet life and substantially changed the Soviet legal climate.

Consistent with the turn toward socialist legality, the number of prisoners held in the camps declined during the post-Stalin years.[7]

Estimates are that there was a convict labor force of 3–4 million between 1945 and 1950;[8] Soviet statistics suggest a tremendous increase in the population of labor camps between 1945 and 1953, from 1.46 million to 2.47 million (Suny 1998, p. 365).[9] In addition, there were 300,000 convicts in regular prisons and at least 2 million displaced "settlers" whom Stalin punished for alleged complicity with the German army during World War II (Suny 1998, p. 365).[10] By the early 1970s the number of prisoners in all Soviet prison facilities was "somewhat higher" than the 1.7 million that Andrei Sakharov had estimated in 1974 (Chalidze 1977, p. 200). As a percentage of the Soviet population, these figures represented a dramatic drop between about 1953 and 1975. Human Rights Watch estimated a total Soviet prison population in 1985 of about 1.6 million (HRW 1991, p. 3).

Debates among Soviet criminologists, though constrained by ideological considerations, were relatively wide-ranging in the 1960s and 1970s. Social problems such as alienated youth, alcoholism, and poverty emerged as contributing factors to lawlessness (Connor 1972). In fact, by the mid-1960s, amid the revival of criminology as an academic discipline in the Soviet Union, criminologists became involved in formal policymaking as part of a general trend under Leonid Brezhnev toward "scientific management" (Los 1988, p. 18). One researcher has contended that a law-and-order approach to crime gave way during this period to "a pragmatic and flexible approach to criminal policy, which transcended the liberal/conservative dichotomy" on the best ways to fight crime (Solomon 1977, p. 69). As a result, flexible approaches to dealing with crime became more prevalent. Incarceration was still widely used as a tool of criminal justice, but other forms of punishment and rehabilitation became widespread as well. Additionally, liberalization within the Soviet court system began to take shape in the late 1970s, which reduced incarceration rates considerably (Fogelsong 1996).

Despite limitations in the data, it is possible to profile the types of crime committed in the Soviet Union from the early 1960s to the beginning of the Gorbachev era. First, crimes against the person, particularly violent crimes like rape and murder, were probably relatively low compared to levels in the United States (though higher than in Western Europe).[11] Second, property crimes, as well as economic crimes against the state generally, were pandemic (Los 1988, chap. 8; Smith 1991, pp. 221–222). Third, most scholars agree that the relatively low levels of violent crime were attributable to the harsh response of the authorities, the severe treatment of recidivism, and restrictions on firearm ownership (Connor 1972; Smith 1991; Chalidze 1977; Shelley 1987). Fourth, crime in the Slavic republics (Byelorussia and Ukraine, in addition to Russia) was high compared to Soviet rates in general.[12] This is attributable to the greater consumption of alcohol in those republics (Connor 1972; Shelley 1987; Segal 1990). Fifth, unlike most urbanized societies, where crime concentrates in the larger metropolitan areas, in the Soviet Union many remote rural areas or newer cities contributed a surprisingly large share of total crime. One scholar (Shelley 1987) contends that restrictions on travel allowed authorities to direct former convicts away from the more coveted living areas such as Moscow and St. Petersburg.[13] The large cities also had much greater concentrations of police.

The trends I am describing pertain to the Soviet response to ordinary criminal justice. Of course, the Soviet regime also persecuted and prosecuted individuals deemed "enemies of the state" for participating in "anti-Soviet agitation." As of the early 1980s, about 10,000 Soviet citizens were under arrest or in prison for specifically political offenses (Los 1988, p. 113). Also, authorities arrested a somewhat larger number of individuals on nonpolitical charges as part of a strategy to harass "nonconformist" activists or political dissidents (Los 1988, p. 113). It is also reported that a total of 6,000 individuals were prosecuted under articles 70 and 190-1 ("the two most explicitly political statutes of the criminal code") between 1958 and 1986, with tens of thousands more between 1967 and 1974 being warned of impending prosecution under those two statutes (Reddaway and Glinski 2001, p. 91). And, of course, the KGB was ubiquitous in Soviet life, monitoring citizens for signs of disloyalty. Further, it is clear that prison officials tended to subject "politicals" to harsher treatment than ordinary criminals (Solzhenitsyn 1974). In the late 1970s and early 1980s, the regime became even harsher in its repression of political dissent; prominent activists of the 1960s and 1970s, including Alexander Solzhenitsyn, Andrei Sakharov, and Lyudmila Alexeeva were either driven into exile or imprisoned. This campaign virtually stamped out the more overt forms of dissent by 1980 (Alexeeva 1984, 1990). Thus, the "progressive" trends in criminal justice of the late Brezhnev period do not apply to political repression.[14]

Beginning in the late 1980s, the Soviet Union experienced a profound judicial transformation. At the Nineteenth Party Conference in 1988, Gorbachev called for sweeping legal reform to ensure the supremacy of the law over the state (Quigley 1989, p. 453). Previously, the Soviet Union had condemned international oversight of state laws—first arguing that such oversight violated sovereignty, then later asserting that countries prioritize different values and that these were not a matter for universal principles to judge (Jhabvala 1985, p. 477). Under

Gorbachev, the Soviets began to soften their insistence that human rights were internal matters. Gorbachev continued to insist, in line with previous Soviet thinking, that social and economic rights were an important priority. However, he contended that these rights were a necessary basis for civil and political rights and that the latter set of rights had to be specifically and actively protected (Quigley 1989, pp. 456–458). On the level of practice, changes came swiftly between 1986 and 1990. In its report for 1986, for example, AI observed "no improvement in the harsh and arbitrary treatment of prisoners of conscience," although, in a harbinger of things to come, the great dissident Sakharov was released in December (AI 1987, p. 320). By 1987, AI was noting that "changes in the political climate of the USSR gathered momentum" (AI 1988, p. 218). Among the notable achievements that year were the Soviet ratification of the UN Convention Against Torture and the confirmed release of 259 prisoners of conscience (AI 1988, p. 219). Significantly, AI noted that whereas actual improvements in human rights were substantial, legal changes lagged behind.

During this period, the number of political prisoners held by the regime continued to dwindle against the backdrop of much more sweeping prison reforms. A mass amnesty by Gorbachev for various nonviolent and political offenses during 1987–1988 reduced the size of the Soviet prison population to about 1 million (HRW 1991, p. 9); the rate per 100,000 persons dropped to about 300. Additionally, HRW reported significant changes in the practices of camp and prison officials. Although conditions remained poor in many respects, the incidence of beatings, torture, and violence more generally appeared to decline during the late 1980s (HRW 1991, pp. 3–8). Economic crimes remained pervasive under Gorbachev, as haphazard attempts at economic reform created an ambiguous legal climate for many kinds of economic activities that were formerly illegal and remained nominally so. The growing economic chaos unleashed during the late Gorbachev period, especially in 1990–1991, led to increased organized criminal activity and crime more generally. These developments must be borne in mind in appreciating the sources of social upheavals that characterize post-Soviet Russia (Vaksberg 1991; Handelman 1995).

However, the adoption of sweeping economic reform in 1992, upon Russia's independence from the defunct Soviet Union, unleashed a new level of social chaos. The ensuing levels of crime, the state response to that crime, and the state's incapacity to manage the burgeoning prison system led to a reversal of the gains under Gorbachev—a reversal so extreme that Sergei Kovalev, Russia's best-known human rights activist and former resident of the Gulag under Brezhnev, was moved to remark: "Stalin was a splendid torturer, but prison life in Russia today may be even worse than it was under him."[15] My intent is not to compare prison conditions today with those of Stalin's Gulag, in which barbaric conditions and summary executions were routine. Rather, I suggest that day-to-day life for prisoners in Russia today is in many ways harsher than it was for Soviet prisoners after Stalin's death in 1953.

Crime and Punishment in Post-Soviet Russia

Crime

Crime in Russia has soared since the late 1980s. Figures compiled by the Russian state statistical committee Goskomstat reveal the extent of the problem. In 1990 there were 1.84 million registered crimes. This figure jumped to 2.8 million in 1993 before falling off slightly. In 1996 the number of officially registered crimes was 2.63 million, more than 40 percent higher than in 1990 (Goskomstat 1997, p. 269). In 1999, total reported crime topped 3 million and continued to increase in 2000 and 2001 before falling off in 2002.[16] As was true in Soviet times, current crime statistics, if anything, understate the true extent of the problem. Police are judged on their conviction rates and therefore have a strong disincentive to register crimes that they might have difficulty solving. Additionally, many citizens, especially women, are reluctant to report certain kinds of crimes because they do not believe that police will take their reports seriously.[17] However, there is no dispute that on the whole crime has increased dramatically since the late 1980s. One strong indicator is homicides (see Table 2.1).

It should be noted that the increase in murders in the Russian Federation began earlier than 1990, given that the figure for 1988 was 10,500.[18] Furthermore, the sources of crime are complex; one focus is the Russian mob. Criminal syndicates—the mafia—largely run out of the prison camps, persisted for decades in the Soviet Union. As many have noted (Connor 1972; Chalidze 1977; Vaksberg 1991; Handelman 1995), these gangs developed their own language, organizational rules, and an alternative code by which to live. An essential part of that code during the Soviet period was total rejection of life on the outside. But the centrality of the Gulag system for the operation of criminal syndicates weakened with the collapse of the Soviet Union (Handelman 1995). The legalization of private business activities, the extraordinary transfers of wealth, and other opportunities for enrichment made available to individuals (i.e., other than those well-placed in the Soviet

Table 2.1   Murder in the Russian Federation, 1990–2001

Year	Total Homicides
1990	15,600
1991	16,200
1992	23,000
1993	29,200
1994	32,300
1995	31,700
1996	29,400
1997	29,300
1998	29,600
1999	31,100
2000	31,200
2001	33,600

Sources: Goskomstat (1997, p. 269; 2003). Shelley (2003, pp. 112–113) contends that Russia's "patterns of homicide more closely resemble those of countries with serious internal conflicts" and suggests that the Chechen conflict, confined to one part of the country, cannot explain the more generalized pattern she observes.

party-state structure) compelled criminal leaders to "step back into society" to run their empires (Handelman 1995, pp. 19–20). Reports on organized crime suggest that mob activities might represent 40–70 percent of Russian GDP.[19] Russian media regularly report on contract murders, complete with graphic pictures of the latest victim. The general sense of lawlessness that pervades Russian life nowadays lends itself to such characterizations. As a result, discussion of the mafia in any analysis of crime and punishment in contemporary Russia is unavoidable.

Yet I give little attention to the mafia, for two reasons. First, the term is too broadly applied, encompassing everything from local hoods who want a "piece of the action" from street vendors to the extraordinary corruption that has accompanied privatization (Clarke and Burawoy 1993; Kagarlitsky 1995; Lieven 1998b; Hoffman 2002). Organized gangs that maintain a hierarchical structure and clear business goals are deeply entwined in the economic life of the country. However, gangs have not produced the same opportunities for corruption created by the free-for-all that characterized the breakdown of the central planning structures and the party-state monopoly on property. Rather, they have fed off any opportunities available to them in the gray world of the Russian economy (Kotz and Weir 1997; Sergeev 1998; Goldman 2003). Thus, as a causal variable in understanding the problem of crime in contemporary Russia, the mafia as an analytical category is almost impossible to tease out from other social and economic processes.

There is a second reason why I do not treat the Russian mob in more detail: discussions of crime in Russia tend to exaggerate the mafia problem. Using the example of murder: various sources estimate that some 500–600 contract murders take place each year (Juviler 1998, p. 150). Many of these, including the murder of the extremely popular TV personality Vladimir Listyev in 1995, made sensational headlines. These figures are minuscule, however, as a percentage of all murders. Additionally, much of the massive increase in reported property crimes is of the petty variety, not related to mafia activity in any meaningful sense.

Punishment

Gorbachev's partial economic reforms during the late 1980s led to breakdowns in the distribution system and to the fabled shortages that undermined his popularity. These breakdowns only strengthened opportunities for illegal or semilegal rent-seeking.[20] This intensified in the form of "spontaneous" privatizations, which accelerated during the late 1980s and early 1990s. This form of privatization occurred when, in the aftermath of the institution of self-financing, enterprise directors achieved de facto, if not de jure, control over the resources and profits of the enterprises under their management. The weakening coercive apparatus under Gorbachev made it more difficult to stop these processes, and well-placed party-state bureaucrats began seizing state property for their own benefit.[21] The problems engendered by the manner in which wealth and power were transferred from the CPSU beginning in the late 1980s persist today. In response, first Boris Yeltsin and then Vladimir Putin launched campaigns to combat the organized crime and corruption that the regimes viewed as undermining Russia's transition to a stable market economy and the rule of law.

Although these are the professed targets of anticrime measures, evidence shows that it is not the mafia that is being victimized by this crackdown. In fact, the mafia is often in league with the police. In November 1997 Interior Minister Anatoly Kulikov acknowledged that authorities remained utterly unable to stem the tide of corruption, fraud, and embezzlement.[22] Additionally, corruption was so widespread among the police that reports of police complicity with organized crime figures became ubiquitous.[23] If the crime-fighting campaign is not having a discernible impact on organized crime, then who is it affecting? Increasingly, it is punishing petty criminals. For example, the MCPR reported the case of a woman held in pretrial detention for months because she stole three cucumbers. A sixteen-year-old boy was convicted and received two and a half years in prison for stealing three hamsters from a pet shop (AI 1997, pp. 26–27). These are not isolated examples. Rather, they follow a policy of maximum incarceration that is the centerpiece of the regime's "crime-fighting efforts," which have caused the population of Russia's prisons to expand. According to MCPR (1996a, p. 4), "instead of reducing the number of prisoners and penal institutions down to the level suitable to the state budget, arrest as a measure of restraint is applied more often, incarceration is the main punishment and a new criminal code stipulates longer terms of imprisonment."

Another notable trend is in the social background of individuals who commit crimes and are convicted for their activity. According to Goskomstat, in 1990, of all crimes committed, about 17 percent were committed by individuals adjudged to have no stable source of income. In 1996, nearly 50 percent of criminals were in such circumstances (Goskomstat 1997, p. 270). Among those convicted of crimes, in 1991, 21 percent were deemed able-bodied and were neither working nor in school. By 1996, that figure had risen to 47 percent (Goskomstat 1997, p. 272). Given that the number of convictions nearly doubled between 1991 and 1996, it seems clear that there is a strong social economic component both to the increase in crime and the class character of its effects on convicts. One Russian commentator noted that "life has pushed many more adult citizens, who had previously not committed crimes, onto a path of crime. The fight for reforms [has] degenerated into a fight for survival" (Bakatin 1995, p. 27). A comprehensive new report on Russian prisons released in 2003 reveals that this pattern persists (MHG 2003).[24]

A further contributor to the growing crime rate has been the increase in alcohol consumption (see Chapter 3) and in the illegal use of drugs. Drug use has exploded among youths since the early 1990s. One indicator is that the number of individuals under thirty arrested for drug-related crimes in 1996 was six times as high as compared to 1990 (Goskomstat 1997, p. 271).[25] The increased consumption of drugs and alcohol is attributable, in large part, to the strains of economic reform. Given the high rate of crime committed while "under the influence," the implications are obvious.[26]

A final point is that many analysts attribute crime, and the responses to it, to inequality in society. According to a report by the Russian Academy of Sciences (RAN), as of 1995 the top 10 percent of the Russian population had fifteen times the wealth of the lowest 10 percent, a figure RAN deemed to have exceeded the maximum permissible norms for law-based states. Goskomstat reports that the average income of the top 10 percent of income earners, compared to the bottom 10 percent, was 4.5 times greater in 1990. In 1992 it was eight times greater, and by 1996 it was thirteen times greater (Goskomstat 1997, p. 138). According to RAN data, that ratio is now 20:1.[27] The relationship between income inequality and crime and lawlessness is certainly more complex than a simple threshold would suggest. However, it seems clear that the unprecedented increase in societal inequality is a contributing factor to the increase in crime as well as to the profile of individuals most likely to be arrested and convicted. The criminologist Marc Mauer (1995, p. 113) suggests that the "relative punitiveness [across nations] may be a function of the degree of general societal inequality." What is beyond dispute is that the large increase in crime and the attendant crackdown on it have serious implications for the conditions in jails and for life-integrity violations against prisoners.

Prisons

In 1991, reporting on the state of prisons in Russia and Uzbekistan, HRW noted substantial improvements in prisons, particularly due to the mass amnesty of 1987–1988. Additionally, HRW noted that in virtually every prison that it investigated "long-term inmates uniformly reported that physical abuse, once common, is now rare," which it partly attributed to the far less crowded facilities and the attendant decreases in stress on both inmates and guards (HRW 1991, p. 4). HRW still regarded prison conditions and prison transport facilities as harsh.[28] It also reported that conditions in pretrial detention centers (SIZOs) were especially severe, primarily due to overcrowding. HRW warned that a significant increase in crime, apparent by 1990, would threaten some of these gains. Evidence from reports by the UN and other advocacy organizations, coupled with the admissions of system officials themselves, confirmed HRW's fears. There are, broadly speaking, two ways in which prison life poses a mortal threat to inmates in Russia: physical abuse and torture, and prison conditions. Both are attributable to overcrowding.

Overcrowding

Overcrowding in Russian prisons is one of the primary obstacles to the realization of nominally granted legal protections. In turn, overcrowding itself has several sources. Until 2001, Russia's prisons held more than 1 million inmates, equal to the number of inmates held in all Soviet prisons at the beginning of 1990.[29] A significant portion of this increase results from the growth in SIZO populations. As of 2001, MHG (2001, p. 218) reported that thirty of Russia's eighty-nine regions had overcrowding in SIZOs of more than 200 percent of capacity. MHG also reported that Russian SIZOs process 1.3 million people per year and that only about a third of those kept in confinement are ever sentenced to prison (MHG 2001, p. 218). One source of the growing populations in the SIZOs is the refugees from the Caucasus, including Chechnya and Dagestan (see Chapter 6). More significant, Yeltsin's Decree 1226 (June 1994) authorized law enforcement officials to arrest individuals suspected of involvement in criminal gangs for up to thirty days without charge. This decree was in direct violation of the Russian constitution, which limits the period of detention without charge to forty-eight hours.[30] Further contributing to the burgeoning SIZOs, suspects in detention are regularly denied the right to legal services, and many detainees are held three to five times longer than necessary while awaiting sentencing.[31] AI notes that bail is rare in Russia, even if suspects are neither violent nor flight risks; "this aggravates crowding in pre-trial detention and, due to delays in bringing cases to trial, results in many suspects remaining in pretrial detention for longer than the maximum penalty they might face if convicted" (AI 1997, p. 6).[32]

Many sources report overcrowding on the order of 300 percent in certain institutions.[33] For example, at Matrosskaya Tishina, a remand center in Moscow, 140 prisoners occupied a cell built for thirty-five. Another dynamic exacerbating overcrowding is the increasing lag between the decision to prosecute and commencement of the trial. Whereas in 1988, 8.6 percent of cases were disposed of in "excess of trial time limits," by 1997, 25.4 percent of cases fell into that category (Solomon and Fogelsong 2000, pp. 117–119). Declining physical plants, inadequate medical care, and worsening diets—characteristic of virtually all Russian prisons—are especially acute in the SIZOs.[34] In conjunction with the physical abuse to which prisoners are subject, the conditions have severe repercussions for the life-integrity rights of prisoners.

Physical Abuse

Regarding the prison conditions during the Brezhnev era, "it appears from the existing documentation that beatings, rapes and torture are the reality which most Soviet prisoners experience, witness or are involved in with the approval of the prison authorities" (Los 1988, p. 118). Such brutality abated under Gorbachev's rule, but violence by prison officials against inmates, partly a result of overcrowding, has apparently increased dramatically since 1992 (AI 1997, p. 2).[35] According to the well-known former dissident Valery Abramkin, now director of MCPR, one explanation is that progressive reforms passed by the old Russian parliament in 1992 deprived prison administrators "of lawful and habitual methods of controlling prisoners" (Abramkin 1996a, p. 5). Abramkin does not advocate a return to Soviet-style methods of prisoner control. Instead, he contends that the reformed laws "were seemingly indifferent to the existing social and cultural reality and to the necessity to count the results of legal effects on a concrete social object" (1996a, p. 5). Specifically, Abramkin warns that in the absence of appropriate resource provision (especially the increase in penitentiary staff), as well as structural changes in the prison system, the new laws were likely to further burden prison administrators. Growing strains on fiscal resources, partly a product of austerity measures dictated by IMF loan conditions, made such reforms unlikely. In this context, when the new laws were not openly ignored, they were often circumvented by more violent and arbitrary methods.

In its 1997 report on prisons in Russia, AI (1997, p. 11) observed that "torture and ill-treatment occur at all stages of detention and imprisonment . . . but is most often reported during preliminary or pretrial detention." One pattern that AI found during its investigation was that, while victims of torture and physical ill-treatment come "from all walks of life . . . those most likely to be ill-treated are the less educated or the less privileged—for instance, ethnic minorities, the unemployed [and] vagrants" (1997, p. 11). Commonly reported methods include beatings on the genitals, imposition of suffocating gas masks while being hung by the hands from a wall or a ceiling, and regular use of fists and feet to interrogate or discipline suspects and other detainees (AI 1997, pp. 16–20). AI (1997, p. 19) speculates that "a general feeling of impunity and state protection apparently experienced by the police . . . is often the reason why innocent people, sometimes no more than passers-by, become victims of torture." It is impossible to quantify the extent of the physical abuse in the Russian penal system, but all observers agree that the problem is pervasive.[36] However, perhaps even more threatening to prisoners are the conditions themselves.

Prison Conditions

Reports suggest that overcrowding is so severe that there is sometimes literally insufficient oxygen for prisoners to breathe, prompting AI and other observers to contend that the conditions, especially in the SIZOs, amount to torture. Nigel Rodley, the UN special rapporteur, wrote of his visit to Russian prisons in 1994: "the senses of smell, touch, taste and sight are repulsively assailed. The conditions are cruel, inhuman and degrading; they are torturous" (1994, p. 151). Yuri Kalinin, then head of the Directorate of Corrections for the Ministry of Internal Affairs (MVD), essentially agreed with Rodley's contention, saying that "conditions in our pre-trial centers, according to international standards, can be classified as torturous—the deprivation of sleep, air and space" (quoted in Abramkin 1996a, p. 3). There is a particularly cruel irony in the conditions of the SIZOs, since "crimes of humanity are being committed by the Russian state against thousands of its citizens, who cannot be considered guilty until a sentence is pronounced" (Abramkin 1996a, p. 3).[37] Due to the overcrowding, inmates sleep in shifts and food is scarce. One inmate reported that "when you're not sleeping you are standing. The prison administrators provide the bare minimum to keep a person alive. We had tea every morning. For lunch watered down soup and porridge, for dinner more porridge."[38]

However, the problems noted above are not confined to the SIZOs. Infectious diseases in prisons have spread dramatically, accompanied by a deterioration of medical services. Vladimir Spetsnadel, the top official for prisons in St. Petersburg and the Leningrad region, claimed that the federal government was sending local prisons 45 percent of necessary medication. Given the catastrophic health crisis in Russian prisons, this last fact is especially disturbing. Tuberculosis rates in prisons are 60 times higher than those in the general population. Recent figures suggest that 84,000 prisoners, or nearly 10 percent of the total, have TB.[39] Of those who are infected, nearly one-quarter have the incurable, multiple-resistant type. Disturbingly, 30,000 infected prisoners are released each year. In addition to tuberculosis, evidence suggests a deterioration of prison conditions throughout Russia.[40] The Kovalev Commission, in its report for 1994–1995, noted that gross violations of Russian law in the prisons were reported in Novokuznetsk, Tambov, Buryatia, and Volgograd, as well as other regions of the Russian Federation.[41]

The amnesties appear to reflect a growing recognition by authorities that the system was economically and socially unsustainable. Abramkin notes that "the resources the government commanded were too limited to support the physical survival of the million prisoners, to say nothing about compliance with at least national regulations. Everything was in short supply, including food, medical services, sanitary and hygienic materials" (MHG 2003, in Fitzpatrick 2003). A persistent lack of funds has plagued the prison system. In his comparative study of prisons in seven Central and Eastern European countries, including Russia, Roy Walmsley (1995, p. 6) notes that the "economic situation . . . means that there is little money for refurbishment and . . . none at all for building new prisons." The reasons for the shortage of funds are complex, and include the sharp reduction in social spending since the onset of economic reform. This has had obvious implications for the ability of government institutions to carry out basic functions.[42] The Kovalev Commission (1996a, p. 40) reported that the prison system received only about 75 percent of funds allocated to it in 1996. According to MHG, a federal upgrading program (Building and Renovating Pre-Trial Detention Facilities and Prisons) has been undermined by lack of funding. In fact, by early 2001 the money intended for upgrading facilities was at 3 percent of the required level to fully fund the program (MHG 2001, p. 219). The shortfalls, including nonpayment of wages to personnel, not to mention the horrendous hazards to which they are exposed on a daily basis, also contribute to growing violence against inmates and have led to an increase in suicides among those who work in prisons (Juviler 1998, p. 151).[43]

In one way or another, then, the lack of material resources in Russia contributes to a catastrophic situation for prisoners generally. However, institutional (as opposed to economic) factors also contribute to the interrelated problems of excessive detention, overcrowding, violence, and mortally threatening conditions. These include decentralization of judicial authority and a lack of horizontal accountability, each of which I will discuss briefly.

Decentralization of Judicial Authority

According to one scholar of Russia's judiciary, Todd Fogelsong, the Soviet Union experienced a progressive revolution in its judicial apparatus during the late 1970s and early 1980s. Beginning in 1980, the regime reduced by half the number of people it prosecuted for petty offenses such as vagrancy and begging. Furthermore, judges meted out lighter punishments, including fines, in place of incarceration for lesser offenses (Fogelsong 1996, pp. 282–286). These changes stemmed from the belief that incarceration led to "disruption of family and other socially useful ties," which in turn would only lead to more crime (p. 290). In the language of the times, Soviet officials viewed criminalization as likely to exacerbate the alienation of individuals from the networks of "mature socialism" (p. 290). Officials also believed that, given the growing fiscal pressures on the Soviet state, which were already evident by the late 1970s, incarceration was a poor use of resources. A further impetus for this change was the accession of Vladimir Terebilov to chairmanship of the Soviet Supreme Court in 1984, a year before Gorbachev came to power. Terebilov believed that local party officials exerted too much influence on trial court judges, usually to convict and impose harsher sentences. Terebilov's accession accelerated an existing trend, which was that the Ministry of Justice and higher courts usurped the authority of the CPSU to oversee judges' work. Under Terebilov's "bullying, harassing, and sanctioning of trial court judges," courts began increasingly to overturn convictions and reduce excessive sentences. Between 1983 and 1987, courts reduced the number of reversals for excessive leniency from 20 percent to 10 percent. During the same period, they reduced sentences in 50 percent of cases (p. 293). These changes occurred immediately prior to Gorbachev's own radical changes.

Therefore, trial court judges became dependent on higher structures of authority during the late Soviet period, particularly under Terebilov. However, because of Terebilov's priorities and his institutional authority, there was substantial improvement seen in incarceration policies (from the standpoint of human rights), in particular the size of the prison population. This hierarchical structure broke down in fundamental respects with the collapse of the Soviet Union. As a result, in conjunction with the severe strain on resources, the judiciary in post-Soviet Russia has become complicit in the incarceration policies of local and federal authorities, with dire consequences for the life-integrity rights of inmates. As the Kovalev Commission (1996a, p. 53) reported, "reform of the legal system is proceeding slowly and spasmodically. The structure, goals and powers of the existing system do not provide an effective defense for the rights of the individual in Russia's complex new circumstances." This report reveals that budgetary constraints undermine the proper functioning of courts. For example, in 1996 the Kovalev Commission estimated that the courts would receive about one-third of the funds considered necessary to function adequately (p. 40). In July 1998, the Constitutional Court ruled that the proposed 1998 budget was unconstitutional because it stipulated further cuts in spending on the judiciary. Citing article 124 of the constitution, the court noted that the federal government is solely responsible for the "complete and independent functioning" of the judiciary, which the court deemed impossible under prevailing budgetary circumstances. Judges regularly go without paychecks, and in many areas courts do not even possess the resources to pay for telephones, electricity bills, and postage to mail subpoenas.[44]

One consequence of this budget-cutting is burgeoning caseloads. This contributes to excessive stays in the SIZOs. While suspects languish in SIZOs, judges are unable to review their cases. Given the widespread policy of "jail first, investigate later," the backlog of cases is a human rights disaster. Additionally, as central judicial structures lose their authority over regional and local courts, federal laws are ignored by local judges. Observers have noted that the judicial reforms of 2002 intended to reverse these trends have changed little. "Courts still depend on executives for funding, so a judge who crosses his governor can have trouble receiving money even for such basics as stationary and envelopes."[45] Judges also have become susceptible to bribes and other forms of pressure, especially due to their poor economic circumstances and the inability of law enforcement to protect them. This is a positive development for incarcerated mobsters but a negative one for most other suspects; regional political authorities put strong pressure on judges to hand down harsh sentences, even for petty crimes (Fogelsong 1996, p. 312). Huge case backlogs, insufficient funding, political pressure, and contradictory laws and court proceedings "lead to red tape, and . . . cripple the defense of the lawful interests and rights of citizens" (Kovalev 1996a, p. 53).

Lack of Horizontal Accountability

There is also the problem of accountability that stems from the resistance of governmental agencies to undertake meaningful reform in conformity with federal law and constitutional requirements. Several observers have noted that government bureaucracies are even more bloated today than they were in Soviet times and that the state machinery is no longer under bureaucratic party control. In the Soviet period, there was accountability of sorts in which governmental agencies were beholden to a central coordinating structure: the CPSU. The relationships between ministries and the party were fraught with corruption. However, a mechanism existed whereby there was some oversight of bureaucratic functions. In other words, if officials failed to carry out certain tasks, punishment could be swift and sure. The desire of officials to maintain certain privileges, which would be impossible without good standing in the party, ensured a degree of conformity with party mandates (Lieven 1998a, p. 214). And when the CPSU collapsed, "party discipline disappeared. Nothing replaced it" (Shelley 2000, p. 96).

Eugene Huskey (1996, p. 329) has explicitly criticized former president Yeltsin for this situation. Huskey contends that repeated calls for judicial reform were thwarted under Yeltsin, partly because the MVD, which controls the police system, would suffer greatly if progressive reforms were carried out. Huskey calls Decree 1226 a "victory" for the MVD over the court system, which was overwhelmed as a result of the decree. This bureaucratic infighting is part of a larger dynamic within the government, what is called *vedomstvennost*, or departmentalism. In the absence of a force, like the CPSU, that could play a coordinating role within government, budgetary and resource allocation struggles become Darwinian contests. Huskey contends that under such circumstances weaker interests, like the courts, tended to lose out (pp. 330–331). This sort of bureaucratic infighting helps to explain the delays in transferring the prison system from the jurisdiction of the MVD to the Ministry of Justice.[46] In all modern polities, bureaucratic prerogatives are an important determinant of resource allocation. What is most disturbing about Russia today is that there appears to be no countervailing influence to such prerogatives or any mechanism for adjudicating among them and limiting them to acceptable channels. Under Vladimir Putin, there have been renewed efforts to impose uniformity on Russia's asymmetrical federalism, including in the area of law enforcement. From the standpoint of human rights, some activists see this as a potentially positive development given that federal laws and the constitution itself are quite enlightened.[47]

Conclusion

In Russia today there has been a revolution in legal reform and a full commitment, on paper, to meeting the most rigorous international norms for observance of human rights laws. But a persistent problem is that implementation of those laws has not kept pace. The presence of observers at institutions all over the country attests to an openness inconceivable in Soviet Russia until the late 1980s.[48] Further, it is impossible to deny the brutality that characterized Soviet prisons, especially before the Gorbachev era, and their failure to meet international standards. It appears, then, that the abuses today are somehow less sinister, in that they are attributable to many factors and there is no single culprit. In other words, there no longer exists a centralized state operating a massive coercive apparatus in willful violation of people's basic rights for expressly political reasons. However, the record suggests that in both its size and in the conditions to which inmates are subject, prisons today are as harsh as they have been at any time since the death of Joseph Stalin; in fact, they are worse in important respects than during the last years of the Soviet Union. Abramkin, once a political prisoner, has said, "When I visited a common cell in Butyrka prison, I felt a deadly horror and realized that the horror I had seen before was a mere trifle. . . . [The tortures of the Gulag] were limited in time: minutes, hours, days, months. Now, prisoners are being tortured for years" (quoted in Juviler 1998, p. 151).

If the process of devolution of central authority leads to a lack of accountability for manifestly acute violations of basic norms, then it is incumbent upon analysts to reconsider their tendency to laud changes away from centralized structures, even those of the notoriously repressive CPSU. Economic reforms in Russia have created a more unequal society in which deteriorating social conditions breed crime. At the same time, budgetary constraints have strained resources in prisons and in the legal-judicial apparatus more generally, undermining the courts' ability to act as independent arbiters of the law. Judicial decentralization has further weakened legal structures. In combination with these factors, local law enforcement officials appear able to act with increasing impunity to deal with crime without regard to federal norms. This impunity is exacerbated by the state's anticrime crusade, which provides a rationale for the excesses that have become so evident in Russia. Furthermore, Russia's war on terrorism, however justified it may be, threatens to further undermine the accountability of law enforcement agencies to basic human rights norms. As a result, the state is too weak to sustain accountable and minimally functioning institutional structures, specifically prisons, as well as a juridical apparatus that might check the excesses of prison or other law enforcement structures. The result has been an appallingly high rate of mortality, with an estimated 16,000 people dying while in prison during the 1996–1997 period alone (Solomon and Fogelsong 2000, p. 151).

It remains to be seen whether the judicial reforms of 2002, including plans for jury trials in all regions of the Russian Federation by 2007, as well as greater constraints on prosecutorial latitude, will have any notable impact on the size and conditions of the prison system. Russian courts currently convict 99 percent of criminal defendants, and the early evidence from jury trials that do take place in Russia is that conviction rates are lower.[49] However, jury trials are also more costly and difficult to coordinate. Whether authorities have the resources or the will to ensure the timely and orderly implementation of this and other reforms is unclear. However, until now Russia has witnessed a kind of selective chaos, a convenient "transitional" stage for federal and local law enforcement and the elected officials and political appointees who are nominally responsible for protecting the rights of citizens. For the large number of individuals placed in Russia's prisons at least since 1992, the result has been misery and death.

Notes

1. "Gulag" is an abbreviation of Glavnoe Upravlenie Lagerei (Main Directorate of Prison Camps).

2. Shelley (1996, p. 3) contends that Soviet law represented a combination of continental European, colonial, and communist practices, all of which subordinate individual rights to state prerogatives.

3. The constitution of the Russian Federation was ratified by popular referendum on December 12, 1993, two months after a violent confrontation between President Yeltsin and his opponents who had rallied around the former vice president, Alexander Rutskoi, and the speaker of the old parliament, Ruslan Khasbulatov. The previous constitution was promulgated in 1978 and had been amended hundreds of times in the late 1980s and early 1990s to reflect the extraordinary changes in Russian society. The 1993 constitution grants a wide range of explicit constitutional rights to citizens, which are regarded as inviolable, except by due process of law. The constitution also obligates the Russian Federation to bring its laws into conformity with those of international human rights treaties of which Russia is a signatory (Russian Constitution, chap. 1, art. 15, no. 4).

4. Two of the more prominent accounts of this type are Waller (1994) and Shelley (1996).

5. For example, Sergei Stepashin, then-head of Russia's Federal Security Service, commented in 1994 that "I am all for the violation of human rights if the human is a bandit or a criminal" (quoted in AI 1997, p. 2).

6. Freedom House, while recognizing the substantial liberalization taking place under Gorbachev, still classified the Soviet Union as "not free" as late as 1990. The Freedom House scores for the Soviet Union were 6 for political freedoms and 5 for civil liberties in 1990 (Freedom House 1991, pp. 251–256). In 1991, for the first (and last) time, the Soviet Union was recognized as "partly free" (1992, p. 471). In 1993, Russia's scores were 3 and 4 (1994, p. 469). As of 1999–2000, it has since dropped back, to 4 and 5, and is still recognized as partly free (Freedom House country scores, available online at www.freedomhouse.org/ratings/phil.htm).

7. Hosking (1992, pp. 327–332) describes a general relaxation of prison-camp regimen that took place during the late Stalin period. Beginning in 1948, prisoner diets began to improve, prisoners could retain a small portion of their work-related salaries, and prison stores were opened where goods could be purchased. One possible motive for this relaxation might have been the growing unrest throughout the camp systems. Many camps saw full-scale rebellions, in which prisoners overpowered prison guards. In some cases, the response was intense repression. However, the situation undermined production targets in many camps, which put local officials in a precarious position. Such relaxation did not apply to "politicals."

8. There were also between 1.9 million and 3.7 million German POWs— a tiny percentage of whom returned home after the war—who were employed in massive projects, such as the construction of the monstrous buildings at Moscow State University and the Volga-Don Canal (Suny 1998, p. 365).

Applebaum (2003, pp. 579–580) also notes that there was extraordinarily high turnover of inmates in the camps, so that the year-to-year figures of inmates underestimates the total number of people passing through the system.

9. Part of the explanation for this may be attributable to a campaign against "improper prosecutions" launched by the procuracy in the late 1940s. In effect, any judge, prosecutor, or investigator who was involved in a case that resulted in acquittal was subject to scrutiny by ministerial authorities. Acquittals, not surprisingly, dropped substantially between 1949 and 1953 (Solomon 1996, p. 236).

10. Gilinski (1993, p. 37) estimates nearly 6 million exiles between 1940 and 1949, though he is including "Kulaks" in his figures.

11. In 1988, early in the perestroika period, there were about 10,500 reported homicides in the Russian Republic (Foreign Broadcast Information Service [FBIS], SOV-095–96, May 18, 1995, p. 27). In 1985, there were about 20,000 murders in the United States (Mauer 1997, p. 9). Los (1988) warns that the catchall category of "hooliganism" in Soviet crime figures masked many more severe interpersonal crimes, such as rape and assault. The prevalence of murder, it seems, would be harder to obscure (p. 287).

12. The three former Slavic republics persist in having the highest incarceration rates of the former Soviet republics (see data collected by the MCPR 1996b and Mauer 1997).

13. Los (1988, p. 105) believes that so-called antiparasite laws, under which people who were not working were arrested, in conjunction with the forced labor of prison inmates, were largely an economic strategy: "a convenient solution to labor shortages in inhospitable but economically important regions." She contends that the completion of many of the largest construction projects resulted in lower rates of incarceration (p. 109).

14. Applebaum (2003, p. 550), citing others, reports that there were 365 victims of psychiatric abuse.

15. Quoted in "One Day in the Life of . . ." *Time International*, May 25, 1998.

16. "Crime in Russia up Twenty Percent," *Izvestia*, May 5, 1999, in *Current Digest of the Post-Soviet Press*, 51(18), June 2, 1999, p. 12. More recent data are reported in *Asia-Africa Intelligence Wire*, February 6, 2003, which notes that the 2002 data represented the first reported drop in five years. Russian Deputy Prosecutor-General Yuri Zolotov expressed skepticism about the 2002 data, arguing that a "semblance of law and order is being achieved largely through manipulation of statistics [which] reflect not the level of crime in the country, but the level at which the state and society counter crime." *ITAR-TASS*, June 5, 2003, from *Johnson's Russia List (JRL)*, June 5, 2003.

17. In April 1998, Prime Minister Sergei Kiryenko and Interior Minister Sergei Stepashin called on police to stop "whitewashing" crime statistics. "Kirienko and Stepashin Call for Truth in Crime Statistics," *RFE/RL Newsline*, April 15, 1998.

18. FBIS, SOV-095-96, May 18, 1995, p. 27.

19. A report presented to former president Yeltsin in 1994 found that

70–80 percent of private banks and businesses in major cities were forced to make payments to organized crime (Kotz and Weir 1997, p. 184).

20. In one sense, the impact of these shortages has been overstated. Production did begin to slow during this period. More acute, however, was the diminishing availability of goods through normal channels. Shipments of bread to local stores would immediately disappear because they were being sold out the backdoor at much higher black-market prices. What this required was connections, or *blat*, to get access to basic items, as well as enough rubles to pay for those items. The criminal syndicates profited enormously by this breakdown in the distribution system. The result was not, however, a crisis in public health or a worsening diet for the average Soviet citizen. There was, however, a massive transfer of wealth from ordinary citizens to individuals who participated in these schemes, not to mention an extraordinary burden on people's time. This latter effect did have important consequences for economic productivity (Menshchikov 1990).

21. This process is described in Kotz and Weir (1997). Sergeev (1998) contends that the first "businessmen" of the perestroika period were government bureaucrats who started private enterprises and developed ties with local law enforcement and regional party bosses to provide "cover" for their activities. These amalgamations were counterweights to the growing activity of organized crime. At the same time, state agencies established cooperatives (the Gorbachev-era term for private businesses), which eventually facilitated the transfer of "colossal public financial holdings to [private hands]" (pp. 76–77). Interestingly, Los (1988) observes that there took place, in both Poland and the Soviet Union in the late 1970s, an increasing concentration in control of wealth and resources in the hands of certain clusters of ministries and bureaucracies, something that she refers to as a "gradual secret privatization" based upon mutual guarantees of various elites.

22. "Tide of Corruption Overwhelms Police," *Moscow Tribune*, November 10, 1997.

23. In the 1997 murder of a suspected "don," it was revealed that several of his bodyguards were police commandos from an elite assault group, whom the Ministry of Internal Affairs had subcontracted out to a shell company controlled by the murdered individual. "Night Job Goes Wrong for Elite Cops," *Moscow Times*, April 9, 1997.

24. A Moscow Helsinki Group report ("Situation of Prisoners in Contemporary Russia") notes that theft has accounted for an enormous percentage of the increase in crime since the start of reforms and that a substantial portion of this subset of criminals are from economically disadvantaged circumstances. The report is available online at www.mhg.ru/english and is summarized by Catherine Fitzpatrick for RFE/RL, "(Un)Civil Societies," June 9, 2003.

25. Recent estimates suggest that there has been a fifteenfold increase in drug addiction. "Russian Health Experts Present Latest 'Shocking Figures,'" from *Obshchaya Gazeta*, reported on BBC Monitoring and *JRL*, March 12, 2001.

26. RAN study, reported in FBIS, SOV-095–066, April 6, 1995, pp. 79–85.

27. Reported in "Russian Society in Critical Condition," *Rosbalt*, April 25, 2003, from *JRL*, April 25, 2003.

28. Valery Sergeev, deputy director of MCPR, told me that conditions in transport facilities represented the one area of improvement within the prison system in post-Soviet Russia that compared with Soviet days. Personal interview, March 14, 1996.

29. The incarceration rate per 100,000 citizens stood at more than 700 until 2000, when a mass amnesty resulted in the release of 140,000–200,000 prisoners. This amnesty dropped Russia to second, behind the United States, worldwide in incarceration rates. However, reports suggest that a high percentage of amnestees have been rearrested, and the general problems of overcrowding and poor conditions do not appear to have been affected by the amnesty (Ana Uzelac, "Doing Time," *Transitions On-line*, March 30, 2001). Subsequent amnesties have included the release of certain women and children and have brought the overall figure down to around 877,000, from a high of 1.1 million. "Reforming Russia's Decrepit Jails," Baltimore *Sun*, June 9, 2002 (Associated Press), from *JRL*, June 9, 2002; MHG (2003); and interview with Victoria Sergeeva, of Penal Reform International, Moscow, January 16, 2002.

30. Yeltsin amended the decree in June 1997 to ten days, although authorities consistently flout the new rules, and many regional authorities have issued decrees similar to 1226, despite the fact that the Constitutional Court has ruled against them. "Constitutional Court Strikes Down Republican Anti-Crime Law," *RFE/RL Newsline*, July 3, 1997.

31. Inaccessibility to legal services is a major problem in Russia; many detainees cannot afford representation, and lawyers simply refuse cases if they are not paid. Interview with Alexander Mironenko, Institute for Penitentiary Reform, June 13, 1996. In July 1998 the Russian Constitutional Court ruled that criminal suspects in pretrial detention must be allowed to appeal their cases, even before sentencing, because tens of thousands had been in pretrial detention for longer than the stipulated sentence assuming a conviction. "Court Affirms Right to Appeal while Criminal Case Is Pending," *RFE/RL Newsline*, July 8, 1998.

32. The new criminal code, which came into effect in 2002, is supposed to provide for bail in a greater number of cases, as well as for alternative sentencing, including community service. Prison officials are aware of the problems of overcrowding and have worked in recent years with human rights activists to develop legislation on the problem. Interview with Sergeeva, Penal Reform International, Moscow, January 16, 2002.

33. Juviler (1998, p. 151) estimated that SIZOs meant to hold 81,000 prisoners held 295,000 by 1996. Alexander Mironenko, of the Institute for Penitentiary Reform, estimates that Butyrki, one of Moscow's notorious remand cells, has held 8,000 prisoners in a deteriorating structure meant to hold 2,500 (personal interview, June 13, 1996). MHG reports overcrowding on the order of 430 percent in Khanty Mansiisky Autonomous District, 350 percent in Tver, 324 percent in the Chuvash Republic, and 321 percent in the St. Petersburg and Leningrad regions (p. 219). Recent amnesties have substantially reduced the population of the SIZOs, though overcrowding remains pandemic to the system.

34. According to the prosecuting supervisor for Moscow at the time, Vladimir Ovchinnikov, inmates had "effectively less living space than any of their predecessors since 1956." Alexander Gordeyev, "Vague Prison Laws Fuel Inmate Abuse," *Moscow Times*, July 22, 1994, p. 3. This was one month after Decree 1226 went into effect.

35. Viktor Orekhov, a former KGB captain who was a political prisoner from 1978 to 1986 after he began calling dissidents to tell them when the KGB was coming to search their apartments, was sentenced to three years in prison in 1995 on a trumped-up gun charge. The arrest was almost certainly motivated by his outspoken criticism of a Yeltsin appointee to the Moscow police force. After an enormous public outcry, Orekhov was released in 1996 after serving ten months. Orekhov told me that he was regularly beaten in prison and estimated that 90 percent of his fellow inmates were similarly treated. He felt that life in the prisons had clearly become more violent than it had been during his earlier imprisonment. Personal interview with Orekhov, July 1, 1996.

36. In its country reports for 1999, HRW notes that law enforcement officials in Russia use torture to extract confessions as an absolute matter of course and that prosecutors simply refuse to investigate such cases.

37. Valery Sergeev, assistant director of MCPR, told me that the awful conditions in the SIZOs serve as an effective investigative tool for the authorities; prisoners will often confess to crimes simply in order to receive a sentence and a transfer to a prison camp, where conditions are, relatively speaking, better. Solomon and Fogelsong (2000, p. 145) similarly note that, as a matter of convenience, pretrial investigators preferred to have suspects locked up so that they could be easily located for questioning and evidence-gathering.

38. "One Day in the Life of . . . ," *Time International*, May 25, 1998.

39. MHG (2003), reported by Fitzpatrick (2003).

40. Recent data released by the deputy justice minister, Yuri Kalinin, estimates that 90,000 inmates have some form of tuberculosis and 36,000 are HIV-positive, in addition to hundreds of thousands who are drug addicts or alcoholics, or suffer from mental disorders. "Over 500,000 Russian Prisoners Sick—Justice Ministry," Interfax, November 27, 2002, from *JRL*, November 27, 2002.

41. For example, eleven inmates died in a prison in Novokuznetsk in July 1995 when temperatures in an unventilated cell reached 110 degrees and officials refused to provide water. The Kovalev Commission (1996a, p. 42) reports that in that same prison in 1994, 100 inmates slit their wrists as part of an attempted mass suicide.

42. Time International reports that Russia's prison budget for 1998 was $1.3 billion, which was less than one-third of the budget for the state of California. Remnick (1999) does not provide figures but notes that prison budgets are slashed every year. The Time International figure does not specify the allocation of money, but what is clear is that the money allocated, though clearly insufficient, is itself a misleading figure, because funds allocated often do not reach their intended destination. Sergeeva, of Penal Reform International, did tell me that since the transfer of prison administration from the MVD to the Ministry of Justice in 1998—finally carried out in 2000—a

greater proportion of allocated funds for things like food and medicine reaches its destination. Personal interview, Moscow, January 16, 2002.

43. Whereas Mironenko and many others cite a lack of funds as a primary cause of the conditions in Russian prisons, the MCPR contends that misuse of funds is more to blame. Valery Sergeev of MCPR says that the government has been spending a growing percentage of its dwindling budget on law enforcement. The problem is that it has been strengthening coercive mechanisms while neglecting basic nutritional and medical standards in prisons. In other words, the problem is the priority of the regime as much as it is material constraints. In 1996 Sergeev told me that, like his director, Abramkin, he did not believe that at its current inmate level the state could possibly maintain the prison system adequately, even if there were no corruption and every ruble were spent wisely. Personal interview, March 14, 1996. As suggested above, the recent amnesties appear to be a belated recognition of that fact.

44. "Court Says Government Can't Economize on Judiciary," *RFE/RL Newsline*, July 20, 1998.

45. The quote is from Matt Bivens, "A Glum Report Card on Russia," *Moscow Times*, June 2, 2003, from *JRL*, June 2, 2003.

46. Critics pointed out that the MVD stood to lose 35 percent of its funding if the transfer took place. The justice ministry long accused the MVD of using funds earmarked for new prisons to build barracks for its burgeoning number of soldiers. "Transfer of Responsibility for Prison System Delayed," *RFE/RL Newsline*, February 26, 1998.

47. Tanya Lokshina expressed this view to me in an interview in Moscow (January 14, 2002). She especially supported efforts to ensure that courts would be fully funded out of the federal budget and said that, regardless of whether human rights protection was Putin's intent, the outcome of such policies would be salutary for human rights and equal protection before the law.

48. As an international election monitor for the Russian presidential elections in 1996, I visited Butyrki prison in Moscow on June 16 and July 3, 1996, to observe whether remand inmates were being allowed to vote. Prison officials were quite accommodating and friendly to the groups of which I was a part, and they frankly acknowledged the terrible conditions over which they presided.

49. Sergei Pashin, of the Independent Council of Legal Experts, reports that the acquittal rate for jury trials in Russia is about 15 percent, but he also notes that there is tremendous systemwide pressure on judges and prosecutors to maintain high conviction rates (Bivens 2003).

3

Violence Against Women and State Indifference

The political science literature on democratization tends to conceive of reform in terms of a public citizen, whose formal rights are the essence of his or her place in a democratic order. Thus, according to the scholarly and popular understanding of democratic transition, the goal of democratization is to bestow rights such as voting privileges, the right to worship freely, and freedom of speech. Regimes that have succeeded in making the transition from authoritarianism to democracy are assumed to have "reformed," or at least to be in the process of reforming, toward less abusive, more free societies based on the formal rights enjoyed by their citizens.

I do not attempt to quarrel over more or less substantive definitions of "democracy." I do contend that during any transition from authoritarian rule, expanding formal political rights may fail to engender expansion of other fundamental rights. In fact, in the chaos of what Michael McFaul has described as a "protracted transition," a fractured body politic may give rise to vast differences in terms of the real abilities of individuals or groups to secure basic rights, even in a formally democratic system. For example, if a Russian law makes it a criminal offense to physically attack another person, but law enforcement officials believe that a man hitting a female partner in the home is not a matter of police concern, then to contend that there exists equality before the law sounds disingenuous, to say the least. Indeed, adult Russian women may be able to vote just as surely as their husbands in elections whose meaning, though problematic, is surely greater than those in which Soviet citizens participated. Yet more of these women are being subjected to more violence than ever, and the evidence suggests that officials are almost entirely unresponsive to these problems. More to the point, women in Russia today find themselves in social circumstances in which their personal inviolability is likely to be trampled in realms in which the state is unlikely to intercede.

In some ways, confronting the problem of violence against women from the standpoint of human rights is more complicated than an analysis of prison conditions. Prisons, like law enforcement more generally, are usually the sole preserve of the state and its agents. As a result, abuses within prisons, even if they flow from neglect or a dearth of material resources, are ultimately the state's responsibility. Any broadly liberal conception of rights would accept that the state has a responsibility to conform to, and enforce, certain basic legal norms in establishing and maintaining prison conditions at a reasonably humane level. However, if individuals confront violence in the home or in the workplace, how exactly is that a human rights issue—even if we feel sympathy for victims of violence in such circumstances? In the next section, I discuss the evolving body of work on human rights law as it pertains to women, especially violence against women. I develop the argument that human rights law grants increasing recognition to the ways in which contexts of power affect the ability of people to enjoy fundamental rights, including rights to physical, or life, integrity.

Violence Against Women and Human Rights

Many feminist scholars have long criticized what they view as a conventional human rights focus that stresses limits on state power, which they claim facilitates the subordination of women to men in the private sphere. An increasing focus on the contexts in which rights are recognized exposes the limits of evaluating equality on the basis of the extension of formal rights by states.[1] In this vein, Charlotte Bunch (1990, p. 490) contends that the greatest restriction to liberty, dignity, and movement (which are universally recognized rights) is the threat and realization of violence. Yet violence in the private sphere, which disproportionately victimizes women, is not regarded as equal in severity to other forms of violence and has not historically been recognized as a human rights concern. Domestic violence is routinely ignored or given short shrift by law enforcement officials, whereas random street assaults are treated as serious crimes.[2] Further, partner-inflicted violence, forced prostitution, and rape, no matter how widespread, have not historically merited the attention that political confinement and state-inflicted torture have (*Human Rights Quarterly* staff review 1991; Reanda 1991, p. 203). Bunch (1990, p. 486) contends that "significant numbers of the world's population are routinely subject to torture, starvation, terrorism, humiliation, mutilation and even murder simply because they are female."

In order to focus attention on grievances that women suffer disproportionately, Bunch proposes a feminist approach for linking human rights to women's rights, one that exposes what she considers to be contradictions in conventional thinking on human rights. For example, if a woman is raped while she is in prison, this will likely prompt attention from advocacy groups like Amnesty International. However, a rape on the streets will be regarded merely as a crime, and a rape in the home may not be acknowledged at all (p. 494). Bunch contends such a prioritization is not the result of natural or cultural processes but rather political ones, in which specific structures of power (i.e., male-dominated) countenance certain kinds of behavior.

In a similar vein, Elizabeth Jelin has criticized what she calls "the excessive formalization of rights" (Jelin and Hershberg 1996, p. 1). Jelin has pointed out that human rights language has historically been couched in terms of equality, neutrality, and the blindness of justice. Thus, it has been difficult to craft legal documents that acknowledge differences (specifically subordination) while at the same time envisioning a goal of meaningful equality. An example of the need to recognize what Bunch and Jelin call context is in the area of domestic battery. Battered women may be physically intimidated or economically dependent or both and thus unable to change their domestic circumstances. And as Bunch points out, sensitivity to social and economic conditions is significant not primarily because those constitute fundamental rights. Rather, the deteriorating economic conditions through which many women are suffering set the parameters within which their very personal safety and basic dignity are undermined.[3] Thus, the level of coerciveness deriving from the battery is qualitatively greater than that from a random street assault, and the terror visited upon women in abusive circumstances that they cannot change should constitute a first-order human rights concern (Bunch 1990, pp. 494–497).

International human rights law does recognize that states' failures to enforce laws equally and to make every effort to mitigate harms perpetrated by some citizens against others represent a violation of states' commitments to human rights under existing treaties. UN documents that recognize women's rights include the International Covenant on Civil and Political Rights (ICCPR), passed in 1966, Convention for the Elimination of All Forms of Discrimination Against Women (CEDAW), passed in 1979, and the UN Declaration on the Elimination of Violence Against Women, passed in 1993.[4] The ICCPR obligates signatory states to "ensure the right to life and to security of person of all individuals within its territory, without distinction of any kind, including sex."[5] CEDAW specifically recognizes that "gender based violence is a form of discrimination which seriously inhibits women's ability to enjoy rights and freedoms on a basis of equality with men."[6] The 1993 declaration reasserts states' obligations to "due diligence," particularly in the realm of violence against women. Significantly, that declaration calls upon states to "prevent, investigate, and in accordance with national legislation, punish acts of violence against women."[7] Furthermore, states' obligations in this matter apply regardless of "whether those acts [of violence] are perpetuated by the State or by private persons."[8]

In sum, the evolution of human rights law takes into account the perpetration of acts that violate fundamental rights in spheres other than those traditionally deemed political or public. This evolution coheres with feminist criticisms of traditional human rights emphases in that it recognizes that the violation of rights necessitates conceiving power and its possible abuse in multiple realms. I would contend that such attentiveness becomes important during a historical period in which the power of private actors is lauded as central to efficiency and happiness, as exemplified by the neoliberal approach to economic reform. In other words, we appear to have a decreasing space in which to speak about public obligation and public accountability. The implications of the growing power of nonstate actors for women may be adverse, and not only in terms of their ability to achieve social and economic security. Crucially, for purposes here, this growing power may embolden private actors to undermine women's personal inviolability at precisely the moment when the state is becoming less willing and able to intervene on women's behalf.

In order to place the problems facing women in post-Soviet Russia in their proper context, I begin with a brief overview of their experience under communism. The rhetoric of sexual equality—a central facet of Soviet ideology—stood in sharp contrast to the reality of persistent sexist mores and widespread discrimination. In fact, many of the patterns of discrimination and abuse that are present today evolved and developed under Soviet socialism. My argument, then, is not that abuse of women's rights and violence against women represent a new feature of Russian life in the aftermath of the Soviet collapse; rather, it is that preexisting forms of sexism have mutated under the post-Soviet transition in ways that have adversely affected women's physical well-being and the will of the state to protect that well-being. The absence of data on violence against women during the Soviet period makes comparisons with contemporary Russia complicated. Therefore, the section analyzing the experience of Soviet women is intended to portray the social circumstances facing Russian women as they entered the transitional period from communist rule to democratization.

Following the section on Soviet women, I address the numerous manifestations of the interaction of Soviet sexism with component processes of the post-Soviet transition to show that the personal inviolability of women appears, increasingly, to be threatened in the new Russia. I contend that democratization studies ignore approaches that focus on the "real distribution of power in society" (Waylen 1994, p. 332). This judgment hampers the study of the effects of the new configuration of power. This is a significant omission because, as Waylen (pp. 332–333) puts it, "democratization at the institutional level does not necessarily entail a more even distribution of power in society, particularly with regard to gender." However, the collapse of the CPSU's role as arbiter of the spheres of work and family life, and the general liberalization of Russian culture and society, have led to an "anything goes" environment, in which preexisting imbalances in power in spheres considered beyond the purview of the state make certain citizens—specifically women—vulnerable to violence.

Before I proceed, one caveat is in order. Describing the situation of "women" as a group does injustice to the age, regional, occupational, attitudinal, and sexual identity–related differences among women in Russia. Recognizing that, my goal is to illustrate how some of the reform processes have tended to jeopardize the physical security of women as women. It is true that women are able to open their own businesses and create nonprofit organizations, which they have done by the thousands; and the increases in violence in society have affected men as well as women, with the authorities being overwhelmed in dealing with all forms of crime. However, given the nature of domestic violence and sexual crimes—that is, crimes against women as women—inadequate law enforcement is likely to have particularly chilling consequences for women. This differing impact is due partly to the male character of law enforcement in all modern societies and the perception, characteristic of liberal societies, that "private" matters should not be of public concern. There can be nothing more threatening to citizens' capacity to assert their most basic rights than constant terror that strikes where one sleeps and is not even acknowledged as terror by those whose duty it is to protect citizens equally before the law.

The Condition of Soviet Women

Equality of the sexes, as is well known, was a basic tenet of Marxist-Leninist ideology. As Barbara Alpern Engel (1987, p. 781) has written, "following the revolution of 1917, the Bolshevik government became the first in history self-consciously to attempt to liberate women" (see also Lapidus 1977; Stetson 1996). Within four days of seizing power in 1917, the Bolsheviks declared an eight-hour workday, applicable to all proletarians, male and female (Buckley 1989, p. 35 and n. 15, p. 59). In 1918, a family code was published in which marriage was removed from the church, couples had the option of choosing either the husband's or the wife's surname, and "illegitimate" children were given a status equal to that of children born in wedlock (Engel 1987, p. 787). Over the next several years, the Bolsheviks passed legislation establishing Women's Bureaus (Zhenotdel), legalizing abortion, easing divorce laws, and assuming state responsibilities for child care and domestic tasks, all of which were designed to facilitate women's entry into the workforce so that they could meaningfully participate in "socially productive labor," something denied to them by bourgeois capitalist regimes (Buckley 1989, pp. 20–27). Interestingly, during the economically trying 1920s the Bolsheviks' response to social stress was to grant women greater legal parity with men.[9] During that decade women were represented in positions of power. Membership of women in the Bolshevik party rose from 7.5 percent of the total in 1920 to 13.1 percent in 1930, and their representation in rural Soviets rose from 1 percent of the total membership in 1922 to 27 percent by 1934; the corresponding figures in urban areas were 5.7 percent in 1922 and 32 percent in 1934 (Nechemias 1996, p. 18). Soviet debate about the transformation of the role of women under socialism was wide-ranging (Stites 1978; Engel 1987; Buckley 1989).

Despite such political gains, individual females' conditions worsened during the economically devastating 1920s. In 1921 the Bolsheviks implemented the New Economic Policy (NEP) in the face of economic ruin brought on by the effects of four years of world war and then three years of civil war. The policy, among other things, introduced market mechanisms and encouraged small-scale private entrepreneurial activity; it also scaled back spending on child-care facilities for mothers and children. The early years of NEP witnessed substantial economic hardship and dislocation, with women suffering a disproportionately high level of unemployment. In this atmosphere, there arose what Buckley (1989, p. 40) calls a "feminization of poverty."[10]

Furthermore, despite their growing numerical representation in official party and government structures, women saw their positions in sites of genuine power diminish steadily in the years after the revolution. From a high of 9.7 percent representation on the Central Committee in 1917, their numbers dropped to 2.9 percent in 1930. Whereas women comprised 16–34 percent of the total of the Supreme Soviet from its inception in 1937 to its complete reorganization in 1989, in the far more significant Politburo, only one woman ever achieved the position of voting member (Nechemias 1996, p. 20).[11] The 1920s witnessed a relatively open discussion about the transformation of women's roles in communist society; however, "official propaganda, avant-garde art, and proletarian culture revealed a world in which women were buxom peasants, farmers, providers, supporters and nurturers" (Nechemias 1996, p. 17).[12]

Once Stalin assumed power, the "woman question" was deemed answered. It was proclaimed that women had achieved parity with men in their roles as builders of socialism, and women's productive contributions to collectivization and industrialization underscored this equality (Buckley 1989). In reality, of course, the period was marked by what can only be characterized as a conservative turn on the question of women. Abortion was declared illegal in 1936 (Buckley 1989, p. 139), and the Zhenotdel were abolished (Engel 1987, p. 788). Although Nikita Khrushchev bemoaned the lack of women in important party positions and was generally committed to greater equality between the sexes, it would not be until the 1960s that the question of the role of women reemerged as a significant issue for debate in Soviet society.[13]

In the two decades before Gorbachev's accession to power, discussion of the double burden carried by women emerged among Western as well as Soviet scholars.[14] Despite recognition of the problems faced by women who must both carry the responsibilities of child care and housekeeping and work outside the home, however, the "solutions" did not involve a shift in gender role expectations. Instead, the Leonid Brezhnev regime attempted to ease women's difficulties by providing generous maternity leave, breaks for nursing mothers, and an extensive network of day-care and health-care facilities (Jancar-Webster 1978, Engel 1987, Buckley 1989). These changes, although undoubtedly better than nothing, were actually part of an extensive pronatalist campaign that emerged under Brezhnev (Bridger 1996; Attwood 1997). Partly spurred by the falling birthrates of non-Muslim Soviet populations (Buckley 1989, p. 15), a sustained media campaign was undertaken that emphasized women's domestic roles and femininity. "Self-sacrifice" characterized a growing educational focus on "natural differences" between men and women, emphasizing women's nurturing qualities and their physical weaknesses while stressing men's bravery, inventiveness, and independent-mindedness (Bridger 1996, p. 23; Attwood 1996 and 1997).

By the time of Gorbachev's rise to power in 1985, the record of

Soviet communism on the question of women was contradictory. Literacy among women, which was an estimated 13 percent at the time of the first imperial census in 1897, was 98 percent by 1959. Infant mortality, 271 per 1,000 live births in 1910, was at twenty per 1,000 in 1990 (Hutton 1996, p. 65). By 1990, women made up 53 percent of the Soviet workforce, the highest labor force participation rate in the world. Women had succeeded in entering, en masse, into many professional sectors in the Soviet Union, dominating certain professions that Americans consider the most prestigious, including medicine, scientific research, and engineering and related technical areas. Life expectancy for Russian women, which was forty-four in 1926, was seventy-six by 1988 (p. 65). By the 1970s, more women were matriculating in institutions of higher education than men (p. 65).

At the same time, despite ideological pronouncements of equality, women were persistently discriminated against in the workplace, through lower rates of promotion, ghettoization into low-paying jobs, and persistent sexist attitudes about what women should, and should not, do. "Protective legislation," first instituted in the wake of the Bolsheviks' 1917 seizure of power, was used selectively to discriminate against women and to hinder their professional advancement, since access to dangerous work was often synonymous with prestige, promotion, and better wages (Bridger 1996; Buckley 1989). The pronatalist campaign initiated under Brezhnev only exacerbated these biases, serving to emphasize that a woman's proper place was in the workplace or the home, not in public life (Jancar-Webster 1978; Lapidus 1978; Bridger 1996). Creeping inflation combined with static wages forced more women to work full-time; yet women were still spending twice as much time on household chores as men (Ardishvilli 1996, p. 105). Scholars have pointed out that the lack of modern conveniences, such as vacuum cleaners and washing machines, a reflection of the command economy's investment priorities, was especially burdensome for women.

When in the 1960s Soviet sociologists began to pay serious attention to the problems of women, they were primarily concerned with discrimination in the workforce, the competing demands on women, the problem of declining birthrates, and, tangentially, the growing problem of alcoholism and its implications for marital breakup. Domestic violence and sexual harassment, always present in Soviet Russia, were scarcely addressed in Soviet sociological sources or in prominent Western analyses of Russian women.[15] This absence stemmed in part from the difficulty in obtaining data, since the Soviet regime bundled domestic violence, for example, under the extremely broad category of hooliganism (Shelley 1987).[16]

The problem of violence against women was also partly masked by the enlightened state of Soviet law in this area. Progressive Bolshevik attitudes toward women were reflected in the Soviet criminal code, first published in 1922. The new code deemed rape a serious offense and gave offenders a jail term of five years, eight under certain aggravating circumstances.[17] It also allowed for marital rape charges by defining rape in the following terms: "sex relations by means of physical violence, threat or by intimidation or making use, through deception, of the helpless condition of the victim" (Stetson 1996, p. 160). Also unprecedented was the code's elaboration of a crime of sexual harassment, which was defined as: "forcing a woman to enter into a sexual relationship or [to] satisfy sex passion in some other form by a person on whom said woman was financially dependent or to whom she was in subordinate position" (Stetson 1996, p. 160). This crime carried a sentence of up to five years. The law's presence on the books at that early date was unprecedented, although the evidence suggests that few people were convicted under this law (Juviler 1977). The problem of domestic violence was simply not a priority for Soviet sociology despite the fact that, as alcohol consumption grew substantially in the 1970s, physical abuse of women, especially domestic violence, became more acute (Segal 1990).[18]

The Soviet legacy, then, was to provide women with unprecedented opportunities for education and work while at the same time insisting, to varying degrees during different historical periods, that they remain the nurturing caretakers that traditional culture asserted was a woman's "natural" duty. Like much else in the late Soviet period, the strains of competing and contradictory demands on women led to increasing dissatisfaction with life chances and material conditions. Increasing emphasis on women's domestic roles at a time and as a result of growing economic stress and social dislocation created conditions in which, I contend, violence against women was likely to become an ever-increasing problem. Therefore, the marriage of Soviet sexism and post-Soviet reform has proved particularly deadly for women.

Post-Soviet Russia

Any account of the rights of women in Soviet society must acknowledge the lack of due process throughout Soviet legal structures. As an empirical matter, women were much less likely to commit or to be convicted of crimes than men (Shelley 1987), but they were certainly not exempt from the arbitrariness and cruelty of the Soviet juridical apparatus. Women also participated in important ways in the Soviet dissident movements that gained international attention from the mid-1960s on (see Alexeeva 1984 and 1990 for discussions of the various tendencies in Soviet dissent). Lyudmila Alexeeva, Elena Bonner, Larisa Bogoraz, and Natalia Gorbanevskaya were among the prominent women in dissident circles. Although the authorities generally treated women less harshly than men (Alexeeva 1990), women were denied basic rights of expression, organization, and association (Alexeeva 1984).

The advent of glasnost and the process of liberalization since the late 1980s have opened a substantial space for the emergence of tens of thousands of independent civic groups. Several thousand independent women's groups lobby, educate, and organize around myriad issues, and women's concerns have gained increasing attention and respectability in the major Russian media.[19] In the legal-formal realm, women, as citizens, have gained the right to vote, organize, and protest, and millions of women have asserted those rights. From the standpoint of a power-based conception of rights, however, the transition has been harmful toward women's rights in important respects. As Dorothy Stetson (1996, p. 163) has argued, "The end of communist rule has been hailed as a victory for international human rights law from the conventional perspective, not a feminist one." I contend that the reforms contribute to a pernicious set of circumstances that is resulting in greater numbers of women suffering grievous bodily harm in a country whose law enforcement agents are indifferent to that fact. There are at least five ways in which reforms and their by-products may be connected to violence:

1. The reforms' negative effects on women's economic and social positions make women more vulnerable to abuse by those individuals in positions of power over them in the job market as well as at home. The threat of unemployment is an example of a social circumstance that creates opportunities for abuse (Gessen 1996). Some scholars also contend that Russia's adoption of a "Western" market ethic, emphasizing individual will, has accompanied the acceptance of an "anything goes" mentality about the market, property, and other people's bodies, with negative implications for sexual harassment and abuse in the workplace (Klimenkova 1994).

2. The reforms have produced a criminalized society, which has led to violence in the home and against women. Crime has increased

dramatically in post-Soviet Russia in purely statistical terms, and the evidence suggests that a large portion of that increase is taking place in the home.

3. The reforms, particularly the austerity model, undermine the ability of state structures to enforce laws, and if law enforcement officials must prioritize which crimes to investigate and which to ignore, then crimes against women often fall into the latter category.

4. The end of the state monopoly on liquor production and the decrease in the price of vodka compared to other basic commodities have led to a tremendous increase in the use and abuse of alcohol (Medvedev 1996). The relationship between alcohol abuse and violent crime is widely acknowledged by Russian law enforcement officials as well as independent experts. More specifically, researchers have long recognized the relationship between alcohol abuse and domestic violence (Shelley 1987; Segal 1990).

5. The relaxation of travel restrictions abroad, generally recognized as an unabashed good, has facilitated an explosion in the compulsory sex trade of Russian women. More generally, prostitution and other sexual services have increased since 1992. This development has led to further violence against women.

These five points represent ways in which liberalization itself—either of an economic or more narrowly political nature (as in the relaxation of travel restrictions)—may have negative repercussions for women's life-integrity rights. This list is not meant to be exhaustive. Rather, these five points provide a basis for developing more fully my contention that particular kinds of economic changes, in interaction with diminishing state capacity, threaten socially vulnerable populations—groups of individuals who are prone to violence in circumstances from which they cannot extricate themselves. In the remainder of this chapter, I will elaborate on these points and relate them to the growing threat to women's personal inviolability in contemporary Russia.

Women's Changing Economic Position

Although women have undoubtedly suffered greatly in economic terms since 1992, the contours of their economic circumstances are more complicated than is often presented by analysts. The percentage of women among unemployed Russians is a case in point. Most sources assert that women in post-Soviet Russia have suffered disproportionately from the emergence of unemployment, arguing that women represent anywhere from 60 percent to 80 percent of the country's unemployed (HRW reports 1995a, 1997b; Attwood 1996, 1997; Bridger 1996; Rule 1996). Scholars have assumed that women are more vulnerable to unemployment because of Soviet era "protective laws" and maternity benefits that remain on the books today. The benefits appear to make women much more expensive now that firms bear a greater share of the social wage than in the past, and the restrictions on engaging in nighttime work or other "hazardous" labor may give employers more incentive not to hire women now that employers have more discretion over hiring and firing than they had during the full-employment Soviet era. However, as Sarah Ashwin and Elain Bowers (1997) point out, although women do constitute the substantial majority of workers who have registered as unemployed with the state, they do not constitute the majority of the unemployed, most of whom do not register for unemployment.[20] Goskomstat figures for 1995 show that in 1992 men comprised just more than 50 percent of those unemployed in Russia; in 1995 men's share of the total of unemployed rose to 55 percent (Ashwin and Bowers 1997, p. 23).[21]

Ashwin and Bowers's point is not to dispute the claim that women have been particularly hard hit by economic changes. They contend that it is precisely women's ongoing commitment to work that makes them appealingly cheap and pliable labor. Employers see women as more conscientious, less demanding, and more likely to do any job, no matter how dirty, compared to men. Ashwin and Bowers describe an "iron law" concerning gender and jobs in Russia, whereby "almost regardless of the physical strength required for a job, if it is low paid and low status it will become a 'woman's job'" (p. 31).[22] These findings do not undermine claims that women have been made especially vulnerable to structural changes in contemporary Russia; Ashwin and Bowers simply emphasize that women do not have to be unemployed to suffer under economic restructuring.

Although Ashwin and Bowers provide an important corrective to some of the looser claims regarding women and employment in contemporary Russia, a close look at other statistics calls some of their conclusions into question as well. It is true that Goskomstat reports that there are more unemployed men than women; however, the composition of the "eligible" workforce itself has changed. In 1992, out of an economically active population of 75.7 million Russians, 72.1 million were employed; of the 72.1 million, 37.1 million were men and 35 million were women. In 1996, the total economically active population was 72.8 million. In that year, 35.1 million men were employed and about 31 million women were employed. The number of economically active men in 1996 was 38.8 million, roughly identical to the number of economically active men in 1992. By contrast, whereas 36.8 million women were considered economically active in 1992, that figure had dropped to 33.9 million in 1996. In other words, although men had higher levels of unemployment in 1996 than women, the contraction of the total labor force between 1992 and 1996 (of nearly 3 million) was almost entirely accounted for by the declining number of women considered economically active (Goskomstat 1997, p. 107).

As of November 2001, according to Goskomstat, approximately 34.1 million women were economically active, while 36.5 million men were in that category (Goskomstat 2001). If Ashwin and Bowers are right to assert that women are still overwhelmingly committed to work,[23] and economic circumstances necessitate finding jobs,[24] those women who have left the workforce may not be classified as unemployed, but this is not the same as saying they wanted to leave the workforce. Many firms force older workers to take early retirement in order to slash costs, and women's retirement is mandated by law to begin five years earlier than that of men (MHG 2000, p. 231). One statistical study (Deloach and Hoffman 2002) suggests that women do spend less time on the job than men. They contend that this is not attributable to the fact that women bear a greater share of the household burden (though they in fact do) or that they are less committed to work than men. Rather, their regression analysis suggests that it stems from the fact that women earn less money than men and are less likely to gain promotions (Deloach and Hoffman 2002).

Goskomstat also reports the circumstances by which people become unemployed and notes that 10 percent more men chose to leave work of their own accord than did women in the years 1992–1995 (1996, p. 95). Possibly, men are leaving unappealing factory jobs for gray-market work that, though not officially reported, can be more lucrative. This may also help explain why fewer men register as unemployed than women: the meager benefits accruing to the unemployed are not worth the time and trouble of registration for those who can do better in a new career underground. If these opportunities are less available for women, then they may have no choice but to take their chances with the state services. These points only add to Ashwin and Bowers's conclusions: ghettoization can mean funneling women into not only poorly paid work but also work through the mechanism of the growing pensionization of women. Given the meager sums that pensioners receive relative to the cost of living, this must certainly be considered an insidious form of downsizing.[25] Ashwin and Bowers (1997, p. 33) believe that "what is likely to happen is that the majority of women will become even more ghettoised than they were in the past, in low-paid undesirable employment, while a small minority might be able to take advantage of the changes."

Women's ghettoization into lower-paying jobs is evident in the statistics on poverty. According to Tatiana Zaslavskaia, a prominent Russian sociologist and early advocate of economic reform during the Gorbachev era, by the mid-1990s the income differentials between men and women became worse. She estimated that of all Russians classified as extremely poor and poor, 71 percent were women. Data for 1996 show that among all urban residents in Russia whose income could be characterized as extremely poor, 87 percent were women.[26] Single mothers are especially vulnerable to poverty; the percentage of single mothers in poverty is nearly twice as high compared to the population as a whole (HRW 1995a).

Other factors have contributed to the increasing precariousness of women's economic circumstances. For example, thousands of preschools and day-care centers have closed since the early 1990s. In 1990, there were about 9 million Russian children in nurseries and kindergartens. By 1995, about 6 million children were in such programs. Furthermore, whereas about 8 million children attended summer camps at the end of the 1980s, by 1995 about half that total did (Silverman and Yanowitch 1997, p. 73). These factors, if they have not forced many women out of the job market, have reduced their ability to compete for some of the more demanding jobs, since women are overwhelmingly responsible for raising children. In other words, women, already suffering from unemployment, are suffering much more from poorly paid work, contributing to their growing vulnerability in the workplace.

One consequence is that many women have been compelled to accept jobs in which they are vulnerable to egregious forms of sexual harassment. Regardless of the existence of progressive laws prohibiting such behavior, sexual harassment is considered widespread, and there is virtually no attempt made to prosecute offenses.[27] Since 1992, partly because of the growing efforts of women's NGOs, there exists much greater awareness of the problem in public than in the past.[28] However, virtually all observers consider the problem worse today, a partial consequence of women's growing vulnerability in the labor market. It is common now for employers to advertise explicitly for female employees who are *byez kompleksov* (without complexes); some ads are detailed about the physical characteristics desired—hair color, body shape, and the like—no matter what the position being advertised (Gessen 1996).[29]

The result is that the burgeoning fashion and makeup industries, and the preoccupation with women's appearances, amid increasing numbers of beauty contests and ads for personal care products in the media, have struck a responsive chord with many women. In combination with traditional Soviet notions about the appropriate sex roles of men and women, and women's growing precariousness in the labor market, these developments create an atmosphere in which women are viewed as sex objects, a likely precondition for harassment in the workplace. However, these traditional attitudes also lead women in Russia to view unwanted sexual overtures by superiors as their responsibility. One study showed that more than half of women polled believed that women's actions and dress prompted the harassment.[30] Lyubov Shtyleva, cochair of the Kola Peninsula Women's Congress, contends that

> in Russia, the problems of sexual harassment in the workplace are similar to the problems of prostitution. They've always existed, but everyone always used to pretend that they didn't. With the transition to economic reforms, the problem clearly got worse. . . . Female employees are often forced to provide sexual services to a firm's clients and its bosses or are forced to have sex when they come to interview for a job. (Shtyleva 1996, p. 20)

Shtyleva (1996, p. 20) also believes that the "anything-goes market has led to anything-goes, quasi-criminal mores." Another problem is that many workplaces, including the kiosks that line the streets of all major Russian cities, pay employees off the books. In these circumstances, in which women work disproportionately, bosses often take workers' passports to guarantee that the employee will not report malfeasances that the boss might commit. The result is that women clerks are "reduced to the status of concubines" (p. 20). Importantly, Russian women generally understand harassment to have occurred only when there has been "actual physical assault, [not] innuendo, verbal insults and the creation of an intolerable atmosphere" (p. 20). In other words, from the standpoint of this study, the widespread sexual harassment I describe would appear to constitute a clear violation of physical integrity. Lewd remarks or other forms of harassment generally are not regarded as such.

In summary, the impact of the economic transformation has had implications for women's economic circumstances and their likely victimization by sexual harassment. According to one Russian sociologist, as a result of economic reform, women have been "channeled into marginal, low-paid, low status sectors" of the economy (Posadskaya-Vanderbeck 1998). This has combined with growing "sexual liberalization," one feature of which has been "unlimited sexual exploitation and commodification of women's bodies" to create work environments in which many male superiors feel few restraints in their behavior toward women. Shtyleva (1996, p. 20) believes that the problem is "by no means sex . . . it's the relationship between the person in authority and his subordinate, in which the boss feels he can humiliate, insult, and psychologically terrorize with impunity." The result has been the pervasive undermining of women's personal inviolability.

Violent Crime

In addition to sexual harassment, other forms of violence against women have increased. The preoccupation with mafia hits and gangland violence obscures the fact that the greatest portion of the increase in violent crime is taking place in the home. Russian law enforcement officials estimate that 80 percent of all serious crimes occur domestically (HRW 1997b, pp. 11–12). The Moscow Helsinki Group (MHG) estimates that close acquaintances and relatives of the victim are responsible for two-thirds of all rapes (MHG 2000, p. 255). Regarding murder specifically, officials, advocates, and scholars have asserted that 14,000–15,000 women are murdered every year by their spouses.[31] It is impossible to verify this figure independently, and the official estimate of the Ministry of Internal Affairs (MVD) is 3,000.[32] The real figure is probably somewhat lower than 14,000. However, considerations of violence between unmarried partners, who are not technically family members, are excluded from the above data and are impossible to obtain. A comparative study of domestic violence in the United States and Russia showed that the gender ratio of spousal homicides was unusually high in Russia compared to the United States and Western Europe, with six out of every seven spousal homicides resulting in the death of the wife (Gondolf and Shestakov 1997, p. 69). Given this high ratio, and based on the dramatic overall increase in murder and the concentration of the increase in crime in the home, one may reliably assert that several thousand more women are dying each year in domestic circumstances compared to the late 1980s.[33]

If discerning trends in the incidence of murder is difficult, then the task of characterizing the trends in rape is that much greater. Goskomstat figures for 1996 show that whereas 15,000 rapes were reported in Russia in 1990, there were just less than 11,000 in 1996

(1997, p. 269). By 2001, the reported figure was 8,200 (Goskomstat 2003). However, given the explosion in all other types of crime, including violent crime, the possibility of an actual decrease in rape is remote, and most who work on women's and human rights issues do not take the rape statistics seriously. Shelters and hotlines for raped and battered women generally assert that only a small percentage of women who are victimized by violence report it to the police. And workers in these fields will state that the general problem of violence against women has only worsened. According to Natalia Gavrilenko, deputy director of one of just two battered women's shelters in Russia, "women [face] worse violence because the times became so stressful. Men suddenly threatened with unemployment, instability, unbelievably high prices and crime on all sides were far more likely than before to take out their resentments on the women at home."[34] Additionally, even when women seek to escape and succeed in escaping marriage, they may still be prey to violence at the hands of their former spouses. Russian law provides that an individual cannot be compelled to abandon a domicile that is legally theirs. A result is that, in many cases, divorced couples continue to live together. Given that many divorces result from alcoholism and physical abuse by the male, these circumstances are especially dangerous for women (HRW 1995a).[35] The growing level of violence in Russia is affecting women in particular, and the almost complete indifference of law enforcement makes this a human rights issue.

Indifference of Police

The overwhelming indifference of law enforcement officials reduces the likelihood of lessening violence against women anytime soon. A 1994 interview given by Yevgenii Riabtsev, head of public relations for the MVD, exemplifies the problem. Riabtsev acknowledged that domestic violence was a serious problem. However, after claiming that women's underreporting of domestic violence was a major cause of the problem, he went on to assert that "after marriage, many women don't look after themselves. They let themselves go physically, and their husbands lose interest" (HRW 1995a, p. 21). This type of insensitivity among law enforcement officials has been widely reported and, given the propensity for violent relationships to escalate, may have deadly implications.

Hotlines that opened in several cities after 1993 have received several thousand calls from women who are victims of violence, including sexual violence. The data from perhaps the best known of the new services, Syostri, a Moscow-based organization that opened in 1994, suggests that rape is massively underreported. Based on Syostri's phone logs, about 10 percent of women report their rapes to police. Of the reports that police do receive, about 20 percent are accepted as crimes and investigated. Based on Syostri estimates, then, 2 percent of actual rapes are accepted for investigation. Finally, of the number of cases accepted for investigation, about 3 percent make it to trial.[36]

If there is a stigma that attaches to rape that deters women from reporting cases to the police, victims of domestic violence are even less likely to speak up for fear of indifference, harassment, and humiliation (HRW 1997b). Additionally, the Russian government does not keep separate statistics on levels of domestic violence, which makes it almost impossible to monitor meaningfully the problem (HRW 1997b). Furthermore, in addition to sexism, stigmas, and the indifference of law enforcement to family-based violence, women may be reluctant to press charges against husbands because of the financial strain that fines and lost income will place on the family. The result, according to Zinaida Batrakova of the Moscow Union of Lawyers, is that "police start to think of [domestic violence] as a joke" (quoted in Bennett 1997, p. A6). One of the most disturbing facets has been the negligence of authorities in dealing with these matters. Part of this negligence is caused by the underfunding of law enforcement agencies, particularly in the areas of sex crimes and domestic violence. Budget cuts and the extraordinary increase in crime lessen the ability of state officials to carry out responsibilities in virtually every realm. Violence against women becomes a low priority. According to Marina Pisklakova, executive director of the Moscow Crisis Center for Women, "It used to be that murder or severe injuries (from domestic abuse) would be prosecuted. But now even murder is not punished or the punishment is very brief" (quoted in HRW 1997b, p. 40). HRW obtained evidence from Saratov, Murmansk, and St. Petersburg in which the police reported very high conviction rates for rape; this high conviction rate, however, is the result of the aforementioned low rate of reporting by police. Unless there is overwhelming evidence to bring a case, the police will not register the crime, let alone investigate it, because they will be subject to unwanted scrutiny by the MVD if they fail to solve crimes at a high rate. Therefore, police have strong incentives to refuse to report crimes if they think they will not lead to a conviction. HRW points out that numerous factors impede the proper processing of complaints of violence, including sexual violence, by women. These include refusal by police to take the complaint; mistreatment of victims; poorly conducted forensic exams and inaccessibility of doctors; and unwillingness to investigate cases even after acceptance of a formal complaint (pp. 21–31).[37]

The problem of police negligence is more acute for sexual crimes than it is for other types of offenses. Indeed, while shortcomings among police departments in vigorously investigating such cases are partly attributable to financial constraints, the underlying opinion that these cases are not "winnable" is based on long-standing biases. HRW's 1997 report contains page after page of testimonials from doctors, prosecutors, and police investigators, both male and female, who insist that in the majority of cases women are at least partly to blame for sexual assault because they were drinking, wore alluring clothing, or agreed to go home with a man (or men). HRW reports one case in which two women were deemed responsible for being raped by four men because they had been drinking, despite the fact that "the two women were held for several days by the men who repeatedly beat and raped them" (p. 19). According to HRW's research, "Law enforcement officials overwhelmingly fail to respond to sexual assault as a crime unless the victim is a virgin, the offender is a stranger, and the violation entails the infliction of visible injury" (p. 19). The combination of constrained resources and the sense that violence against women "is socially acceptable in Russia" contributes to a situation in which "if [the police] do not totally dismiss what [women] say, they treat [the women] like they have betrayed their husbands. They will rarely investigate a complaint unless the woman has been murdered."[38]

Alcoholism

Rape and domestic violence are not new features of the Russian landscape. However, Russian society is more violent today owing partly to the growing incidence of alcoholism among Russian men. Boris Segal (1990) exhaustively studied the problem of alcoholism in Soviet society; another researcher (Lapidus 1978, p. 255) writes that "Soviet analysts cite alcoholism as the single most important cause of marital dissolution."[39] Indeed, virtually every scholar who has studied issues of family and divorce in Soviet times has regarded alcohol as a central source of strain, as well as violence, within the family, and of growing crime from the 1970s onward.[40] It is interesting to note that several sources report a dip in crime overall between roughly 1986 and 1988 (e.g., Serio 1992; MCPR 1996; Nemtsov 1995). This dip exactly coincides with Gorbachev's crackdown on the sale and consumption of alcohol, which has been derided as a misguided policy by nearly all commentators on the period (Hammer 1990; Smith 1991). In other words, whatever the adverse economic consequences of the alcohol campaign under Gorbachev, it appears to have reduced the level of violence in Russian society. Since the abandonment of that campaign in 1988, alcohol consumption in Russia has increased sharply; researchers have contended that this has had dramatic consequences for life expectancy and public health generally (Medvedev 1996; Nemtsov 1995). The most dramatic spike appears to have taken place between 1992 and 1993. In 1993, there was a 75 percent increase in fatal alcohol poisoning.[41] Two likely factors explain this change. Both are related to the fact that "shock therapy" was launched at the beginning of 1992. First, as prices for alcohol became cheap relative to other goods after the onset of price liberalization, consumption went up. Second, as the reforms plunged people into poverty and uncertainty, drinking became more prevalent as a response to stress (Nemtsov 1995, p. 21).

It is also the case, for a variety of reasons, that avenues for recourse among battered women have been closed off in several respects. As Gavrilenko notes, "In Soviet days at least there were authorities that battered women could complain to—their employer, their local party organization or the trade union representatives. They could ask the bosses to influence their husbands to behave better" (quoted in Bennett 1997, p. A6). These channels existed partly because the party's concern with heavy drinkers' work-related problems might lead them to intercede, for purely instrumental reasons, in alcohol-plagued families.[42] The state's retreat from certain spheres, like the family, allows alcohol-induced violence freer rein.

The Traffic in Prostitution

Another way in which women experience violence is also relatively new: trafficking in prostitution. Prostitution existed under Soviet rule; by all accounts, however, the level of prostitution is much greater today. Leaving aside questions of legality or morality, and recognizing that many Russian women rely on sex work as a source of income, from the human rights standpoint it is unacceptable for an individual to be compelled, by threat of physical violence or inescapable economic circumstances, to engage in practices in which she would not otherwise engage.[43] According to the International Labour Organization, forced labor (or involuntary servitude) is defined as "all work or service which is exacted from any person under the menace of any penalty and for which the said person has not offered . . . voluntarily" (1957 Forced Labor Convention, quoted in Caldwell et al. 1997, p. 54). Such "work or service" includes the compulsory sex trade, a facet of the sex industry that has grown as a direct result of the Soviet collapse and the relaxation of travel restrictions.

In a report published in November 1997, researchers for the Global Survival Network (GSN) wrote that since 1991 "a growing commerce in human beings has arisen between Russia and the former Eastern Bloc, on the one hand, and Asia, Western Europe, and the United States, on the other. Russian women are in high demand in many countries because of their 'exotic' nature and relative novelty in the sex market" (Caldwell et al. 1997, p. 8). In part because of women's poor economic circumstances in Russia, the allure of job opportunities overseas is strong. Typically, a woman searching for overseas opportunities will turn to a firm that "specializes" in such placement. Agents for these companies "strike a deal . . . and promise to advance the cost of the airline ticket and arrange for the international documentation, with the understanding that they will be reimbursed once the woman or girl begins working" (Caldwell et al. 1997, p. 18). Typically, women will arrive in a country on a work visa registered as dancers, waitresses, or other such professions. However, they will commonly have their passports taken by the sponsoring agency and become, basically, indentured servants. When they stay in the visiting country beyond the expiration date of their papers, they are no longer legal visitors, although they cannot return to Russia because they have no passport. As a result, they are left to "work off their debt," which the trafficking agencies set at arbitrarily high levels. GSN found that trafficking networks in Russia and elsewhere in newly independent states charge women up to U.S.$30,000 for providing them with "services." Once the women become so indebted (a fact often kept from them until they are overseas) they have little recourse. They are now at the mercy of their "employer/benefactor." During the course of its investigation, GSN discovered that the Russian government is generally uninterested in doing anything about these practices. In fact, bureaucrats are often in cahoots with traffickers, helping to provide false documentation for underage girls who, because of their virginal (and therefore presumably disease-free) status, are in high demand overseas (Caldwell et al. 1997, pp. 12–14).

In early 2003, the Russian Duma drafted legislation that would criminalize trafficking of humans for exploitative purposes. This came on the heels of growing pressure from Russian activists and international organizations. Current estimates suggest that 150,000 women may be trafficked abroad, half of whom are forced into the sex industry. In fact, the industry has become so lucrative that Yelena Mizulina, a member of the Duma, asserts that "income from human trafficking now exceeds the income from drug trafficking."[44] Whether the Duma's initiative will have any discernible impact on the trade remains to be seen. The issues that are manifest in sexual slavery exemplify the more general problems facing women in post-Soviet Russia: dire economic circumstances and desperation in the job market, coupled with a liberalization of laws and practices and an inability or unwillingness on the part of law enforcement to enforce the laws that relate to violence or general exploitation of women. This confluence of circumstances caused one close observer of trafficking to comment that it may be "impossible to stop this phenomenon which is deeply rooted in the economic system."[45]

Conclusion

The extraordinary stress and social dislocation brought about by the reforms, the breakdown of the rule of law, and the diminishment of resources available to law enforcement—along with a Soviet legacy of sexism and strongly traditional attitudes toward gender roles—have combined in a noxious way to undermine women's physical security in post-Soviet Russia. The removal of full employment, far from liberating women from the double-bind of Soviet life, has only added to their vulnerability to predatory employers and to discrimination in the workplace. Liberalization has also spawned the rapid growth of the sex industry, which women are forced into in ever-greater numbers due to precarious economic circumstances. Furthermore, the social stresses of reform have induced an increase in alcohol consumption, with inevitable consequences for violence inside the home. As feminist scholars have pointed out for decades, domestic tyranny overwhelmingly victimizes women and tends to be a low priority within a democratization process that is male-dominated. The devolution of the state's power, heralded as an important step in the direction of democratization and economic reform, means that women will be less likely to be protected by the law. "Anything goes"—the mantra of contemporary Russian reform—has led to cruel consequences for women, for whom freedom, in addition to the right to vote, peaceably assemble, and start their own businesses, means the freedom to fend for themselves in a violent society.[46]

A centralized state may uniformly constrain the behavior of most citizens, but the absence of such constraints, in the presence of other conditions, mirrors the economic imbalance stemming from the reforms. Abstract freedom becomes empty when viewed as a competition among groups for the exercise of their rights and interests. A state that cannot, or will not, level the playing field in this regard effectively weighs in on the side of the powerful. The state is no longer the sole source of repression; it is now merely an unindicted coconspirator in a much more diffuse, though no less pernicious, social process. In Chapter 4, I sketch the circumstances of three socially vulnerable groups (orphans, dark-skinned residents of Moscow, and conscripts) who, like prisoners, are more direct victims of state or parastate agents.

The relationship between economic reform, declining state capacity, lack of horizontal accountability, and the violation of the personal inviolability of Russians is generalizable to a wide range of social contexts and socially vulnerable groups. In extending my argument to these other groups, I show that the problem of violence as a human rights concern appears to reach virtually every segment of Russian society.

Notes

1. Both AI and HRW began producing reports on women's rights in the early 1990s, something that AI, in particular, had resisted doing for many years. Issues such as genital mutilation, wife-beating, the international sex-slave trade, preferential provision of food and shelter to boys and men over girls and women, and the right to "gainful" employment have all received recognition from human rights organizations, in international documents, as well as in the scholarly literature (Thomas and Beasley 1993).

2. This problem is, of course, not unique to Russia. See HRW's 1991 report on violence against women in Brazil, in which the familiar problems of police indifference, attribution of blame to victims, and sympathy for men committing "crimes of passion" are all in evidence (cited in Thomas and Beasley 1993, pp. 51–53).

3. Rebecca Cook (1993) has contended that structural adjustment, and the "austerity" model more generally, have adverse consequences especially for women in developing countries. She notes that under recessionary conditions, the decline in social services burdens women because of their disproportionate responsibility for child care. She also notes that IMF preconditions pay scant attention to the preexisting problem of gender inequities in the workplace, a consequence of which is their likely worsening under restructuring (pp. 242–243).

4. The Soviet Union ratified the ICCPR in 1973 and CEDAW in 1981, and Russia obligates itself to all international treaty commitments established by the Soviet Union (HRW 1997b, p. 14). The 1993 declaration "is a non-binding resolution that establishes an international standard" (1997b, p. 15, n. 54).

5. ICCPR, arts. 2, 6, and 9 (quoted in HRW 1997b, p. 14). HRW points out that the same rights are protected by the European Convention for the Protection of Human Rights and Fundamental Freedoms, to which Russia is also a signatory by virtue of Russia's admission to the Council of Europe in 1996 (1997b, p. 14, fn. 46).

6. CEDAW Recommendation no. 19, para. 1 (in HRW 1997b, p. 15, n. 49).

7. Declaration on the Elimination of Violence Against Women, art. 4c (quoted in HRW 1997b, p. 15, n. 56).

8. Ibid.

9. Engel (1987) notes that an estimated 7 million Soviet children were homeless in the mid-1920s, and the Bolshevik response was, among other things, to ease divorce laws in order to make it easier for women to take custody of children. Farnsworth (1977, passim).

10. One of the results was an epidemic of abandoned children, whose fathers were often not responsible for financial support after divorce (Buckley 1989, p. 40). Until the marriage laws were reformed in 1926, women who were in "unregistered" marriages were more vulnerable to this phenomenon. See also Farnsworth (1977, pp. 138–165) for a discussion of the 1926 marriage laws and the debates those laws sparked.

11. Elena Furtseva served in that body from 1957 to 1961 (Smith 1991, pp. 98, 114).

12. For a discussion of the portrayal of women in Soviet iconography, see Waters (1991, pp. 225–242).

13. See *Soviet Sisterhood,* the edited volume by Holland (1985), for discussions of this development.

14. Among the better-known treatments of the double burden and the evolving role of women under "developed socialism" are Jancar-Webster (1978) and Lapidus (1978).

15. Lapidus (1978) and Jancar-Webster (1978), who have written two of the most exhaustive accounts of women under communism, scarcely mention these issues. Lapidus does briefly mention the relationship between male drinking and marital breakup (p. 255).

16. Soviet crime statistics included various categories for what are called *bytoviye* (which roughly translates as "domestic violence" or, more broadly, crime carried out against the background of ordinary life circumstances). These categories did not differentiate violence against women in the home from violence against men or children; in any event, the statistics were suppressed (Semenoff 1997, pp. 52–56).

17. These circumstances included when the victim was a minor, or committed suicide following the rape, or was raped by more than one individual.

18. Moses (1996, p. 72) contends that one reason for the growing migration of women to urban areas after World War II was that increasing numbers were fleeing from alcoholic and abusive husbands.

19. For example, in 1994 the well-respected daily *Nezavisimaya Gazeta* began running a women's page once weekly devoted to social problems, including domestic violence.

20. Most sources, including Goskomstat (the State Committee for Statistics), use International Labour Organization methodology to estimate real unemployment. In 1996, unemployment was estimated at 9.2 percent of the working population based on International Labour Organization methods, compared with 3.6 percent based on registration with the Federal Employment Service (Silverman and Yanowitch 1997, p. 97). Unemployment rose dramatically during the late 1990s. Alongside economic growth, unemployment has

returned to the level of the mid-1990s, at about 9.3 percent as of February 2003 (Goskomstat 2003).

21. More recent data suggest this pattern has persisted. Data from early 2000 show that whereas women represented two-thirds of those individuals who registered as unemployed, they represented only 45 percent of the actual unemployed (MHG 2000, p. 231).

22. Aleksandr Sabov notes that although 400 occupations are closed to women for supposed "safety reasons," "it's no coincidence that in heavy labor the majority of 'orange vests' are women. The existence of such declarations in legislation, declarations that sound humane but don't have any economic backing, essentially limits women's access to the labor market instead of guaranteeing them the right of free choice" (in *Rossiiskaya Gazeta*, March 6, 1998, in *Current Digest of the Post-Soviet Press* (*CDPSP*) 50, no. 10 [1998]: 17. In other words, "protective legislation" gives employers the option of indiscriminateness in the hiring and firing of women but does not enforce any "protection" of women from hazardous occupations.

23. Qualitative research by Ashwin and Bowers (1997, p. 27) found that of the women they interviewed in Samara, Kuzbass, and Syktyvkar, most find work "crucial to their sense of identity" and otherwise very valuable to them as individuals.

24. Some studies show that only about 5 percent of Russian women could afford to be full-time homemakers (from *Trud*, January 20, 1998, reported in *CDPSP* 50, no. 3 [1998]: 16).

25. In 1991, pensions represented 49 percent of the average wage; in 1996 they represented 35 percent of the average wage. And since pensions are calculated on the basis of earned income, women's pensions are lower than men's (Silverman and Yanowitch 1997, p. 73).

26. Zaslavskaya's data are summarized in Silverman and Yanowitch (1997, pp. 66–67). The 1996 data are from Caldwell et al. 1997, p. 15. The Russian government establishes a subsistence minimum, which it then uses to calculate benefits, but many critics have contended that official poverty estimates are based on faulty assumptions. Vitaly Golovachov contends that the Moscow regional government itself assumes that the minimum subsistence income is 50 percent higher than that calculated by the federal government for dispensing social welfare. The central government developed its method based on the assumption that people could go without buying things like clothes and shoes for an "emergency" period during the first eighteen months of reform in 1992–1993, but five years later the government had still retained the "emergency" assumptions (from *Trud*, October 10, 1996, in *CDPSP* 48, no. 44 [1996]: 18).

27. According to Masha Gessen and others, up to 1990 Soviet courts heard about twenty to twenty-five cases a year under article 118, the section of the criminal code dealing with sexual harassment. In 1990 eleven cases were heard before Soviet courts, five of which occurred in Russia. In 1991 Russian courts heard four cases; in 1992, one case; and in 1993, zero cases (Gessen 1996, p. 2). Since then, there have never been more than eight cases filed in a given year. John Varoli, "Sexual Harassment, Russian Style," *St. Petersburg Times*, March 9, 1999, from *Johnson's Russia List* (*JRL*), March 9, 1999.

28. An American, Martina Vandenberg, a well-known feminist activist in Russia, noted that only beginning in 1995 had male officials, particularly in Moscow, actually uttered the words in public, acknowledging sexual harassment as a serious problem. Personal interview, March 18, 1996.

29. This growing commodification of women's appearances, and the extension of this problem to the labor market, are complicated by the relationship of Russian women to the messages of the Soviet regime. Beth Holmgren (1995) has written that Soviet women often rejected Western feminism and its stress on liberation of women from the demands of the home. For Soviet women, burdened by their high participation in the workforce—despite their domestic chores—the home was often seen as a refuge from the imposed responsibilities of public life. In addition, the image of the commodified woman was "valorized by both political censure and material lack. . . . [I]n the absence of a capitalist market [Soviet women's] extreme preoccupation with looking feminine . . . and obtaining hard to get make-up and stylish clothes signified a personalized triumph over state imposed norms and consumer priorities" (p. 22). Marina Leborakina, a prominent Russian feminist, told me that Soviet women always felt great pride in how good they could look relative to the resources available to them. Personal interview, June 15, 1996.

30. Russian Academy of Sciences sociological study, cited by Varoli (1999).

31. The Russian government gave the figure of 14,000 per year in early 2002 (*Off Our Backs*, May–June 2003, pp. 6–7).

32. Phone conversation with Martina Vandenberg of HRW, May 7, 1998.

33. Andrei Sinelnikov, project director at ANNA (No to Violence), estimates that 12,000–16,000 women die each year at the hands of their partners. From Martina Vandenburg, "We've Still Got a Long Way to Go," *Moscow Times*, March 7, 2001, from *JRL*, March 7, 2001.

34. Quoted in Vanora Bennett, "Russia's Ugly Little Secret," *Los Angeles Times*, December 6, 1997, A1, A6.

35. A 1999 UNICEF study found that in Moscow one in three divorced women had been beaten while they were married (Vandenburg 2001).

36. Data is from an e-mail correspondence between myself and Irina Chernenkaya of Syostri, June 2, 1998. Vandenburg (2001) reports similar findings for the Lana Crisis Center in Nizhny Tagil, where an estimated 2 percent of women managed to get the police to take their complaints.

37. Another way in which inadequate resources impinge upon the proper administration of justice is that Russia's limited forensics resources seriously impede rape investigations, because medical examiners' offices are badly understaffed throughout the country and forensics specialists are preoccupied with autopsies. Therefore, rape investigations, which are to be carried out by the same doctors, are a low priority (HRW 1997b, pp. 25–26).

38. The quote is from Marina Pisklakova of the Moscow Crisis Center for Women, quoted in "Russia's Battered Women Find a Voice," *Irish Times*, March 15, 1997.

39. Hammer (1990, p. 270) cites alcoholism as "responsible for a high incidence of wife abuse and . . . a major cause of divorce."

40. Shelley (1987, p. 42) has contended that crime in the Soviet Union

was characterized by "a greater proportion of [criminal] offenders [who] are either intoxicated or individuals with serious drinking problems." Gondolf and Shestakov (1997, p. 70) estimate that 60–75 percent of male-perpetrated spousal homicides involved drinking by the male. Other figures suggest that 80 percent of murderers are not sober at the time they commit the crime (Nemtsov 1995, p. 21).

41. Medvedev reports that in 1992 Russia ranked first in the world in fatal alcohol poisoning. He also contends that the near-doubling of suicides in Russia between 1988 and 1993 can be partly linked to alcohol. Medvedev (1996, p. 10) contends that Yeltsin's removal of "all controls on the sale of alcohol [in 1992]" meant that "no other country in the world [had] ever experienced such freedom in the sale of alcohol." Other studies indicate that deaths from alcohol poisoning continue to be a serious problem. See "Alcohol Deaths Rise Sharply," *RFE/RL Newsline*, August 28, 2000.

42. Official concerns with drinking and its effects on productivity provided women with a mechanism for pleading with local party officials to shake up abusive, alcoholic husbands by throwing men into "detox" tanks if they persisted in obnoxious behavior. The goal was not to stop wife-beating, necessarily. However, it was a form of intervention, if temporary, that is foreclosed now. Phone interview with Martina Vandenburg of HRW, May 7, 1998.

43. Reanda (1991) criticizes the persistent characterization of prostitution as a victimless crime. She cites a UNESCO study showing that the majority of prostitutes have been victims of rape or other forms of physical abuse and further notes that the real issue is the underlying economic circumstances that compel so many women to sell their bodies to make a living. Reanda contends that prostitution must be viewed as a part of a process by which "the destruction of a woman's identity [is] an essential step in subsequently transforming the human body into a sexual item of merchandise for commercial purposes" (p. 204). Kevin Bales, a prominent researcher on modern slavery, defines the phenomenon as "the total control of one person by another for the purpose of economic exploitation." His work focuses on numerous forms of slavery, including trafficking in prostitution globally (Bales 1999, p. 6).

44. For estimates of the number of Russian women trafficked abroad, see "Moscow Targets Sex Trade at Last," *The Guardian*, February 20, 2003, from *JRL*, February 20, 2003. Mizulina's quote comes from "Want Ads for Slaves," *Trud*, February 19, 2003, from *JRL*, February 19, 2003.

45. The quote is from Elena Turukanova, of the Institute for Social and Economic Studies of the Russian Academy of Sciences, in Paton-Walsh (2003).

46. It is worth noting that as of 2001 there were about fifty domestic violence or rape crisis centers around Russia, which represents remarkable growth over the previous five years. Furthermore, survey data show that large majorities of both men and women consider family violence to be a crime. Women's NGOs and some of the mass media have worked hard to publicize these issues in an attempt to change societal consciousness around violence against women. I have not focused on these developments because, as of now, they have had no discernible impact on levels of violence against women, or on police responsiveness to the problem (Vandenburg 2001).

4

The Victimization of Other Socially Vulnerable Groups

Chapters 2 and 3 explored the context in which life-integrity violations are growing for two population groups within Russia: prisoners and women. In Chapter 4, I extend this argument to socially vulnerable groups who are victimized in the public sphere. Orphans, particularly those in state orphanages, military conscripts, and dark-skinned Caucasians in Moscow are subject to regular, often physically violent, harassment at the hands of police.[1]

Here again I elucidate the relationship between economic reforms and growing social discord, which has begotten a violent society. As in the previous cases, I will show that socially specific violence is a product of aspects of economic reform and the consequent dissolution of accountability. Importantly, the implications of this growing violence are not random or primarily attributable to organized crime. Rather, individuals in socially vulnerable contexts are susceptible to violence due to state indifference, incapacity, and the consequent lack of accountability of situational authorities. In this chapter I provide shorter accounts of the effects of economic and political changes during the post-Soviet transition in order to provide a fuller picture of the pernicious and pervasive ways in which social position makes certain groups of citizens prone to violence despite laws designed to protect them.

Orphans

According to Mikhail Danilin, deputy chairman of the Duma committee on women's and children's issues, the crisis in the number of homeless children in Russia is a throwback to the early twentieth century, when abandoned children could regularly be seen roaming the streets of Russia's major cities.[2] The increase in the number of homeless children must be seen against a backdrop of deterioration in children's well-being, with many suffering from birth defects, malnutrition, and developmental problems (Mironov 2002). Furthermore, homeless children suffer significant levels of violence. For example, one study suggested that 15 percent of homeless children interviewed in Moscow reported being assaulted by police.[3] Most of the homeless children in Russia are regarded as social orphans: they have living parents who for some reason have given up caring for their children. A smaller population of children lives in the system of orphanages that the government maintains. Although mindful of the general deterioration in the circumstances facing children, I will highlight the conditions confronting children in state orphanages. In many ways, the problems evident in Russian orphanages today mirror those in Russian prisons, in which existing resources are inadequate to meet the growing population, the spread of disease, violence, and mortality.

State Orphanages

The opening paragraph of HRW's 1998 report "Abandoned to the State" states:

> It is seven years since the declining Soviet Union released the last of its most renowned political dissidents, and closed a chapter of notorious human rights abuse in psychiatric hospitals and GULAG prisons. Yet today, in another archipelago of grim state institutions, the authorities of the Russian Federation are violating the fundamental rights of tens of thousands of innocent citizens: children abandoned to state orphanages. (HRW 1998b, p. 1)

HRW reports that Russian children, from the moment they are left in state institutions, become victims of long-held prejudices that all abandoned children are in some way "defective." One source of this assumption is the tradition that infants born with severe congenital defects have often been abandoned in local maternity wards under pressure and warnings from the medical staff that the family will be ostracized for raising a disabled child. Even if abandoned infants do not display severe physical or mental disabilities, however, they often come from families with chronic social, financial, or health problems—including alcoholism. These children cannot escape the stigma applied to that past. As HRW (1998b, p. 5) points out, the consequences of this early labeling are profound, "plac[ing] them in an underclass," which then imposes "systematic disadvantages . . . which violate their fundamental rights to survival and development."

The Swiss-based Comité pour la Dignité de l'Enfant published a report in 1995 outlining the criteria by which Russian professionals performed psychological evaluations. In addition to using a strict rubric for evaluating children, doctors record "factors in the child's medical history which would be considered as 'risk' factors in the West, but commonly become labels of illness for an abandoned Russian child" (quoted in HRW 1998b, p. 4). According to the 1995 report, these include:

- babies born to alcoholic parents or whose mothers suffered depression during pregnancy will be labeled encephalopathic and remain so until they come of age;
- orphans will be classed as being mentally deficient; and
- children with a single physical malformation (a harelip or speech defect) become subnormal in the eyes of Russian doctors.

Abandoned children who are diagnosed as mentally retarded[4] "carry that label in their official dossier from institution to institution. They have virtually no channels through which to seek a reassessment or reversal of this diagnosis, and even 'mild' oligophrenics who graduate from technical training schools . . . [have] difficulty appealing for the word to be removed from their file" (HRW 1998b, p. 8).[5] As HRW has documented in some detail, once consigned to state care, orphans live in often squalid and brutally violent conditions that could be termed "Dickensian" (HRW 1998b, p. 22). The mortality rates for orphans in these institutions vary widely by type of institution, and because three different ministries share responsibility for the orphanages, comprehensive and coherent data are essentially impossible to find. However, experts estimate that mortality rates among children in the psycho-neurological homes (*internaty*) are two to three and a half times greater than for children in the general population (HRW 1998b, p. 22). The Mironov report details a litany of serious abuses directed at children in *internaty*, suggesting that the problem is systemic (Mironov 2002). It is true that this population would be at higher risk to begin with, regardless of condition of care, but according to UNICEF's 1997 report *Children at Risk*, the rates of malnutrition, rickets, and anemia increased between 1989 and 1994, suggesting a deterioration in conditions that may be contributing to higher mortality rates.[6] Although comprehensive data for the Russian Federation do not exist, data from Ukraine give some picture of the extent of the problem. In Ukraine's homes for its most severely disabled children,[7] data for 1996 suggest that approximately 30 percent of the children will die before age eighteen, which professionals in the field describe as a "staggering" figure (HRW 1998b, p. 23).[8]

Cultural predispositions appear to play an especially important role in Russia's approach to abandoned children, and this fact must be acknowledged in any account of the conditions facing orphans in post-Soviet Russia. Since the collapse of the Soviet Union, there has been an enormous amount of legislation affirming children's rights to education, health, and special protections designed to shield them from the harsher effects of economic changes. Additionally, in 1990 the Soviet Union became one of the first countries to sign and ratify the UN Convention on the Rights of the Child. In its response to Russia's second report to the UN General Assembly concerning the rights of children (the UN Periodic Report), the UN notes that Russia has, in fact, allocated substantial sums of money since the mid-1990s to improve the quality of children's homes (noted in HRW 1998b, passim, and in "Consideration of Reports" [UN Periodic Report] 1997, para. 53). All of the above suggests that since 1990 Russia has taken notable steps to improve the situation of children in state-run institutions and that to the degree that problems persist they are attributable in part to long-standing practices dating to Soviet times.

However, as I have contended in other contexts, the plight of orphans in contemporary Russia stems from the way in which prevailing patterns and practices mutated under the impact of economic reform and social upheaval into ever-more dangerous social circumstances. According to Russian statistics, in 1992, the first year of "shock therapy," 67,286 children were abandoned by their parents. In 1996 and 1997, that figure had jumped to more than 113,000 per year. The Mironov report suggests that 100,000 new orphans are registered each year (Mironov 2002). UN data indicate that the number of registered orphans increased from 426,000 in 1992 to more than 572,000 at the beginning of 1997 (UN Periodic Report 1997, para. 205). By 2001, according to Moscow Helsinki Group, there were 678,000 children left without care in the Russian Federation (MHG 2001, p. 205).[9] The implication of this is that substantially greater numbers of children are being placed into dangerous circumstances, where the chances of premature death or serious threats to bodily integrity increase dramatically. According to the UN, "The rapid transformation of the social structure, taken in conjunction with the economic crisis . . . has [led to] . . . disorganization of the family, increased domestic violence, including violence towards children, deviant behaviour on a wider scale and, in consequence, neglect of children and social orphanhood" (UN Periodic Report 1997, para. 23).[10]

HRW's report notes that there are significant differences among state institutions for children in Russia today. For example, there are 252 baby houses for orphans up to age four (HRW 1998b, p. 21). In these institutions, observers have noted some palpable improvements since 1992, owing to the increases in donations of toys and other goods from private charities and foreign donors. Additionally, conditions in any institution depend on the director. Some directors are energetic and genuine advocates for the children under their charge, and the conditions and outlook for children in such places can be good relative to those under Soviet rule. However, HRW notes that a negative aspect of decentralization is "an absence of accountability between central and local jurisdictions" such that impunity for directors and staff at the harsher institutions is the norm (HRW 1998b, p. 23).

At age four, children living in the baby houses are given a battery of physical and psychological tests, upon which their lives to age eighteen (and beyond) depend. Those who are deemed normal, or only slightly impaired (*debil*), are sent to children's homes run by the Ministry of Education. These homes allow children to receive the state-mandated nine years of schooling. Conditions in these institutions are difficult but variable. However, if at age four a child fails the diagnostic evaluation of the Psychological-Medical-Pedagogical Commission, she or he falls into the hands of the closed institutions run by the Ministry of Labor and Social Development. These "psycho-neurological" homes (the *internaty*) evince the worst conditions in Russia's state system for children. According to HRW, children in these institutions are routinely "confined to cots in lying-down rooms, often laid out on bare rubber mattress covers, unclothed from the waist down and incontinent" (HRW 1998b, pp. 27–28). Children in these homes who are deemed discipline problems or are potential runaways are "confined to dark or barren rooms with barely a place to sit. The Staff tether[s] them by a limb . . . and restrain[s] others in makeshift straitjackets made of dingy cotton sacks pulled over the torso and drawn at the waist and neck" (p. 28). Especially disturbing is the practice of denying what, in the West, would be routine corrective surgery to children with disabilities[11] based on a long-held bias "against spending medical resources on children judged as 'socially useless'" (p. 28). This social bias is exacerbated in contemporary circumstances by the spiraling costs for medical procedures, which increases the incentive of directors and staff at financially strapped institutions to deem a procedure unnecessary or a waste of resources. In fact, according to the extensive interviews HRW conducted with directors and staff at numerous orphanages throughout Russia, "the staff and directors . . . laid the blame for human rights violations

. . . on the nation's financial crisis" (p. 68). As is the case in the prisons, the financial impact on state institutions, though real, is not always straightforward. Misallocation of funds and outright corruption bear some responsibility for the horrible conditions in prisons and orphanages, as well as in the military.

A final disturbing element is the prevalence of violence as a means of discipline, including the notorious use of punishment by proxy, whereby orphanage staff members assign older, stronger kids responsibility for meting out "discipline" to other children. Such punishment, often referred to by orphans as *dyedovshchina* (hazing), bears a strong resemblance to the kind of discipline enforced in prisons and in the military. And as HRW notes, the word, which is often translated as "hazing," "is understood by Russians as malicious and even deadly" and "is not to be confused with the typical roughhousing among fraternity brothers at universities in the United States" (HRW 1998b, p. 111). The recourse for child victims in state orphanages is minimal, because directors' powers are nearly absolute, and subordinates who report on abuse or corruption risk being fired. The fact that directors keep all files means that they can "doctor" any case in which there might exist implicating evidence against them or their staff.

Each year, according to available statistics, 15,000 Russian children leave the state orphanage system. Of these, an estimated 40 percent become homeless, 40 percent commit crimes, 30 percent are drug addicts, and 10 percent commit suicide.[12]

Resource Pressures and Human Rights Violations

The conditions apparent in Russian orphanages today do not represent a break with a halcyon past. In fact, charitable contributions have improved physical surroundings in many institutions, particularly the baby houses for abandoned children. Additionally, the Russian press has reported critically on abuses in orphanages, which has led to closures of egregiously mismanaged institutions. The greater attention that orphanages now receive, a product of glasnost and the political transformations, allows for the exposure of conditions that in the past were not open to scrutiny.

However, the poor conditions during Soviet times have been exacerbated by economic and social crises. As with prisons, the orphanages (an already poorly run, abusive system) have suffered under the impact of fiscal austerity, growing corruption, and a haphazard decentralization of authority that, while benefiting some children in some institutions, has left others at the mercy of officials and staff. The fact that more children are entering orphanages under such circumstances virtually ensures that abuse and neglect will continue to increase. The progressive changes in legislation, and public discussion of the plight of abandoned children, have not always translated into practice because the state is incapable of implementation and enforcement. According to Lyudmila Yareva, head of the children's house at a prison for women, only the charitable contributions of local businesses provide her with enough food to feed the sixty-four children under her charge. Yareva also points out that funding became a problem only after 1990, when "democratism or whatever you call it" took hold.[13]

Advocacy organizations, like Soldiers' Mothers and the Committee for the Rights of the Child, have urged the Duma to pass legislation (specifically, the law on Public Control Over the Observance of Human Rights in Closed Institutions). Activists see this legislation as crucial in dealing with the lack of accountability of state authorities charged with responsibility for the problems facing children. Clearly, the proposed law, which has languished in the Duma, would also apply to other cases discussed in this study, including prisons and the armed forces.[14]

Arrests of Caucasians and Dark-Skinned Individuals

Russia is an ethnically diverse country with well over 100 distinct ethnic-linguistic groups. Ethnic Russians comprise about 82 percent of citizens within the Russian Federation and are predominant among its educational and political elites (Juviler 1998, p. 163). During the Soviet era, the fourteen non-Russian republics were forced to endure the Soviet leadership's brand of colonialism and ethnocentrism: the Russian language was the lingua franca, and ethnic Russians settled in all parts of the country, assuming leadership positions in local party organizations throughout the republics. Ethnic-national identity was subordinate to the creation of the "new Soviet man" and the building of socialism, which should ostensibly have transcended ethnic identity.

Once Mikhail Gorbachev signaled the introduction of glasnost in Soviet media, nationalism in the non-Russian republics (and eventually in Russia itself) became a potent force. One consequence was the outbreak of ethnic-based conflicts in several former Soviet republics, including civil wars in Tajikistan and Georgia and an interrepublic military conflict between Armenia and Azerbaijan. These conflicts in turn produced an extraordinary number of refugees within the former Soviet space.[15] In addition to the refugees produced by ethnic conflict, the extreme economic hardship evident within the former Soviet Union, especially along Russia's southern borders, has produced a stream of migrants from Georgia, Azerbaijan, Tajikistan, and areas that lie within the Russian Federation itself: Chechnya and Dagestan. Though individuals from these areas are of ethnically diverse origins, they tend to have darker skin than ethnic Russians and are often viewed through similar prejudicial conceptions.

This section will focus on the discrimination that such migrants (and those of similar ethnic origin who have been living in Russia for long periods) face at the hands of Russian regional authorities because of their ethnic backgrounds. Discrimination against "dark-skinned" people or individuals of Caucasian origin has been especially notable in Moscow. Therefore, this section will focus on police abuses in that city. However, law enforcement officials in southern Russian cities, such as Stavropol and Krasnodar, have also routinely harassed and beaten suspected "illegal immigrants" from the aforementioned areas in increasing numbers. And in fact, racism has become so serious a problem that a group of ambassadors wrote a letter of complaint to Foreign Minister Igor Ivanov in May 2002.[16]

In general, the discrimination and violence that these dark-skinned migrants face exemplifies the extent to which the federal commitment to international law and its own constitution is hollow. Regional authorities, unfettered by federal checks, carry out gross violations of the law with impunity.[17] Furthermore, critics have pointed out that President Vladimir Putin's reliance on great power rhetoric, and his reassertion of the notion of national pride, have exacerbated the problems of racism and that Russification has again become a priority for national elites surrounding the president. Finally, the second invasion of Chechnya, the ongoing barbarity of that conflict on all sides, and the 2002 hostage-taking in the Nord-Ost theater in Moscow have led to further persecution of Chechens, or those who look like Chechens, throughout the Russian Federation.

Moscow

Moscow has become perhaps the most popular destination for migrants from other parts of the Russian Federation and from other countries of the Commonwealth of Independent States (CIS) more generally.[18] This is because Moscow has been an island of relative prosperity within a sea of economic turmoil.[19] Moscow's leaders themselves justify their "need to maintain residence and visitors' restrictions and to enforce a policy of no refugees by pointing to a need to achieve zero population growth in the city" (HRW 1997a, p. 3). Moscow's capacity for restricting immigration into the city is itself a product of the continuing *propiska* (internal passport) system; it was to be abolished with the end of Soviet rule but remains in effect today. The *propiska* system provides that all residents of a city or region within Russia must be registered with local authorities within three days of arriving. Following court rulings that forbade localities from denying citizens of Russia the right of residence anywhere in Russia, this system was to have ostensibly been transformed into no more than a "notification" system.[20] Additionally, since Russia is a signatory to all major international human rights instruments, including the ICCPR, it is bound to respect the rights of all individuals recognized as refugees by the UN High Commissioner on Refugees to reside and travel freely anywhere in the Russian Federation (HRW 1997a, p. 2).

The reality is different. Independent human rights monitors, dozens of reports in the Russian press, and testimony from countless individuals all suggest that Moscow police routinely harass and beat dark-skinned individuals (primarily men) on the grounds that they are in violation of Moscow's residency laws. In addition, Moscow's own laws and practices concerning suspected illegal immigrants explicitly contradict federal law and Russia's constitutional and international commitments. Moscow's powerful mayor, Yuri Luzhkov, is popular and receives great credit from Muscovites and outside observers for Moscow's economic prosperity. He also rules in a corrupt and personalistic manner and has made Moscow his private fiefdom in important respects. The abusive practices of Moscow law enforcement are largely attributable to the impunity that he grants his police officers. In this sense he exemplifies the perils of decentralization without accountability that characterize Russian political life today.

Typical Practices

All individuals, whether Russian citizens, asylum-seekers, or temporary visitors, are supposed to carry identifying documentation on their person at all times. Police routinely stop and check individuals to ensure that they have registered with the appropriate authorities in accordance with standing Russian practice. According to the Moscow City Passport Directorate, police carried out 1.5 million document checks on Moscow's streets in the first half of 1997. Of these checks, half resulted in some sort of fine or other sanction for improper documentation. About 60 percent of those cited were from the CIS, that is, from outside the Russian Federation (HRW 1997a, p. 17). A disturbing aspect of this practice is the degree to which individuals with dark skin are likely to be stopped. For example, HRW reports that visitors from Africa may be stopped between five to ten times each day. MHG observes that "one can see the police stopping people daily motivated by [a] single reason—their non-Russian appearance" (MHG 2001, p. 431). It is also routine for people with valid papers to be fined anyway, often after their papers have been torn up. Furthermore, it is standard practice for police not to give out receipts when they collect "fines." One result is that an individual may have to pay fines several times in one day, because he cannot prove that he has already paid another police officer.

These patterns are justified in the name of economic prosperity and for security reasons. However, it seems clear that one purpose is to allow officers to supplement meager salaries by preying on individuals who endure the harassment solely due to their skin color. In its 1995 report, HRW documented the extent to which victims of police harassment reported police use of racial insults in the course of document checks. The use of the term *churki*, which roughly translates as "stupid darkie," is an epithet reserved for dark-skinned non-Slavs in general and is commonly used by police (HRW 1995b, p. 19).

The racially motivated patterns of harassment, and the arbitrary and extralegal way in which fines are assessed, are disturbing enough. However, the use of violence during routine document checks, and the frequent arrest and confinement of individuals for violations of document laws, are commonplace. As in other areas, data simply do not exist to quantify the prevalence of violence by police against dark-skinned individuals. However, anecdotal evidence suggests that the problem continues to worsen. Beatings on the streets and in police stations are common, and the police routinely raid the homes of suspected illegal residents. In these cases, city security is the given justification. However, even if authorities can cite a legitimate justification (e.g., high crime rates or the threat of Chechen commandos infiltrating Russian territory), the result is that law enforcement officials regularly abuse citizens' basic rights without providing any evidence to link them to the alleged crime.[21]

Internal Security

Moscow has been a magnet for internal and external migrants for economic reasons since Soviet times. This pattern has intensified since 1992 because of the greater freedom of movement across borders and because Moscow's relative wealth is greater now. In addition, there have been several security problems in the capital since 1992. The first took place in 1993, when President Boris Yeltsin disbanded the old parliament and, after a tense two weeks, used military means to end the standoff. That conflict, political in nature, had no apparent connection to ethnic conflict. However, Mayor Luzhkov used the pretext of state emergency in Moscow to detain or expel tens of thousands of individuals alleged to be illegal immigrants (HRW 1995b, p. 7).

Moscow authorities have specifically targeted individuals of Chechen origin. One reason is that Chechens (and other individuals from the Northern Caucasus) are suspected of involvement in organized crime.[22] In addition, tension inside Russia peaked during the twenty-month war following Russia's invasion of Chechnya in 1994. During that conflict, Chechen commandos carried out two daring raids on Russian cities, taking scores of hostages and outmaneuvering the much larger Russian army. Then, in May and June 1996, a series of bombs exploded on Moscow's public transportation system. One bomb, on a Moscow metro line, killed four people. Following these attacks, which took place within a week of the first round of Russia's presidential elections, Moscow and federal authorities deployed thousands of extra regular police and military conscripts amid the tense atmosphere. The series of bomb blasts, which resulted in perhaps 300 deaths and shook Russia to its core in the summer of 1999, prompted a new round of harsh treatment of "suspects" of Chechen origin.[23] These blasts were among the primary proximate causes of the decision to invade Chechnya for a second time, in October 1999. Recently, the seizure of the Nord-Ost theater by Chechen commandos in October 2002 prompted further crackdowns on Chechens in Moscow. Matthew Evangelista (2002, p. 73) has also suggested that Putin bears a personal enmity toward Chechens, stemming from an incident in which a Chechen called him a "bastard."

Though no evidence was ever produced to link the 1999 bombings to Chechen terrorists, it was assumed that the attacks were carried out by Chechens.[24] This prompted yet another dragnet of dark-skinned and, particularly, ethnic Chechens by Moscow police. In July 1996, Mayor Luzhkov appeared on NTV, the country's largest independent television station, and engaged in a conversation with a high-ranking police official. During the conversation Luzhkov said, "Now we have to take actions. We have to take out of Moscow . . . the whole Diaspora." The response of the police officer was: "if you only allow us—I will certainly introduce terror on the streets" (quoted in AI, "Urgent Action Appeal: Ethnic Chechens in Moscow," July 22, 1996).[25]

This conversation has to be understood as hyperbolic bluster. However, it is emblematic of an attitude toward Chechens, tens of thousands of whom continue to be, according to international law, legitimate refugees from military conflicts in which Russian forces have inflicted the overwhelming majority of casualties and prompted much of the refugee flight. The conversation also indicates that the racism evident in police actions in Moscow has the approval of the highest authorities in the city. This is especially significant because the Moscow Migration Service (MMS) does not report to federal migration authorities. Rather, the MMS reports only to city officials. As a result, Luzhkov and his administration are not accountable for their migration policies—despite the fact that the size of the fines and the conditions under which police may punish individuals contradict both federal law and all relevant human rights standards and instruments pertaining to refugees and asylum-seekers.

One disturbing but representative example of police impunity took place on April 23, 1996. Ten members of a special unit of the police, the OMON, entered the apartment of a Chechen refugee family in Moscow. Without producing any papers, the policemen began to beat the father and the son while accusing them of involvement with a secret group of Chechen commandos. The police then took the pair away, and it was not until April 30 that the woman of the household discovered that her husband and son had been taken to a prison run by Moscow's Ministry of Interior, where they were being held without charge.[26] In Chapter 2, I noted that law enforcement officials used Decree 1226, ostensibly intended to fight organized crime, to arrest thousands of individuals with no apparent links to criminal gangs of any kind. Under Decree 1226, authorities could imprison individuals for thirty days without charging them, a direct violation of the Russian constitution, which requires that suspects be brought before a court for arraignment within forty-eight hours. This decree was used to imprison Chechens, other Caucasians, and dark-skinned individuals more generally. Once in remand centers, these individuals were subject to all the depredations I outlined in Chapter 2.

Federalism and Racially Based Persecution

As I noted earlier, arbitrary and racist enforcement of internal passport laws, which Russian courts have deemed unconstitutional, is not specific to Moscow. Evidence suggests that similar patterns of behavior exist in St. Petersburg as well as in the southern regions of Stavropol and Krasnodar. In the latter two areas, HRW contends, "ethnic minorities—especially ethnic Caucasians—became scapegoats for the continued economic hardship suffered by most of the population because of the collapse of the command economy" (HRW 1998a, p. 3). This fact, combined with the proximity of these regions to the strife-torn Northern

Caucasus, has spurred patterns of racist enforcement of residence requirements in the wake of the large number of refugees who have come from the conflict zones. What seems clear is that in the realm of local residency laws there is virtually no federal oversight; federalism thus has pernicious implications for dark-skinned residents.

Despite a series of court rulings that progressively weakened residence and registration requirements, there is no evidence that local authorities are changing policy accordingly. Economic scapegoating, the desire to protect a precious economic resource (namely, the right to live and work in Moscow), and public concern with organized crime have provided a pretext for authorities to deny individuals fundamental rights to free movement and residency.[27] Although many of the abuses I describe here do not constitute life-integrity violations, the blatant racism, selective enforcement of registration laws, and physical violence fit many of the same patterns. These include the impunity of decentralized authorities (in this case, geographical) to apply the laws as they see fit in the context of economic and social strains that provide justification (however thin) for clearly illegal acts.

Military Conscripts

One of the most profound changes in post-Soviet Russia has been in the size, strength, and readiness of the armed forces. Once among the most powerful and well-funded in the world, the Russian military has degenerated since 1992. According to Alexei Arbatov, deputy chairman of the Duma committee on defense, "Not since June 1941 has the Russian military stood as perilously close to ruin as it does now" (Arbatov 1998, p. 83). Many factors contributed to this demise. One is the breakup of the Soviet Union, including the dispersal of equipment and weaponry among the former Soviet constituent republics. According to one scholar of Russia's military, Anatole Lieven, the collapse of the Soviet Union and the dismemberment of its armed forces left Russia with a fragment (albeit substantial) of the Soviet military, rather than a truly Russian army, and this has undermined the cohesion of the military (Lieven 1998a, p. 274).

More important has been the impact of fiscal austerity on the Russian military budget. According to Igor Sergeev, Russia's former defense minister, as of December 1998 one-third of all military hardware was not combat-ready, 60 percent of the strategic missile system had exceeded by many years its service life, and two-thirds of aircraft could not fly. In addition, the army does not have the funds to purchase new submarines, tanks, combat planes, artillery pieces, or helicopters. In fact, the air force has not received a new plane since 1992.[28] Overall, the estimated spending level for Russia's military in 2000 was U.S.$6–7 billion.[29] However, the military, like most of the state apparatus, simply never receives all of the funds allocated to it. Data for 1997 suggest that Russia's military received 41 percent of planned levels for medical services, 23 percent for clothing and equipment, and 50 percent for food. In all, the armed forces received just 56 percent of targeted funds.[30] In late 2002 the government announced that it would increase military spending for 2003 by 50 percent, with a large portion of that increase earmarked for pensions and officers' wages.[31] However, ongoing doubts persist as to whether earmarked funds will be allocated, let alone reach their intended destination.[32]

In addition, conditions facing military conscripts have been affected by the general military deterioration. According to the chairman of the Duma's committee on veterans, Valentin Varennikov, the food rations for soldiers in the army and navy were funded at 39 percent of the budgeted levels.[33] As a result, malnutrition among conscripts has become a severe problem and has led to an explosion of crime among conscripts and officers. It has also led to ubiquitous reports in the Russian press about half-starved conscripts begging for food in the towns and villages where they are stationed.[34]

As in Russia generally, corruption plays a decisive role. In 1994, the reporter Dmitri Kholodov was blown to pieces by a suitcase bomb while he was investigating high-level corruption in Russia's military. His chief target was General Matvei Burlatov, whom he accused of pilfering millions of dollars in allocated funds to accounts overseas. A secondary target of Kholodov's investigation was a longtime Yeltsin ally, Defense Minister Pavel Grachev, whose reputation for unscrupulous behavior was so great that he was regularly referred to as "Pasha Mercedes" in popular accounts of his activities. According to Lieven (1998a, p. 283), the allocated money for the military (roughly $15 billion in 1996 and 1997) should have been enough to sustain the army at a minimal level of competence. Government officials themselves have admitted that allocated funds do not necessarily reach their intended destination, although it appears difficult to ascertain just exactly where the money does end up.[35]

Another factor undermining the cohesion and morale of the military is what the former general and parliamentary military advocate Lev Rokhlin described as institutionally induced infighting among the various branches. In terms similar to Eugene Huskey's conception of *vedomstvennost* ("departmentalism"; see Chapter 2), Rokhlin contended that "all these departments are pursuing their own narrow interests. There is no single administrative organ over them which could counter certain leaders' ambitions" (*Rabochaya Tribuna*, August 23, 1996, in Lieven 1998a, p. 288). An example of this kind of infighting is that the MVD has taken on more military functions (in order to increase its power and its budget) despite the fact that it is unprepared to carry out military operations. Its increasing focus on military tasks has also undermined its ability to fight crime, its primary mission. Many officers and other observers see "departmentalism" as part of a political strategy of divide and conquer—an indifference to the overall effectiveness of state institutions in service to certain favored (and consequently loyal) bureaucracies (Lieven 1998a, p. 289). And despite Vladimir Putin's efforts to strengthen the armed services and to consolidate the state bureaucracy, events in the war in Chechnya suggest that substantial changes have not taken place since Yeltsin left office.

Lieven contends that Yeltsin's buildup of border forces and interior troops at the expense of the army led to a decline in morale throughout the armed forces. Combined with extreme malnutrition and poverty among conscripts, one outcome has been the destruction of internal cohesion within units and the growth in violence within the military (Lieven 1998a, p. 274). Stories of killing sprees by conscripts against peers appear frequently in the Russian press.[36] According to official statistics, some 1,100 recruits die each year for noncombat reasons—including disease, suicide, and *dyedovshchina* (hazing)—and that figure appeared to be higher in 2003.[37] Advocates for conscripts and independent sources believe that official statistics undercount the extent of the problem. Soldiers' Mothers, for example, a leading Russian human rights organization, estimates that several thousand recruits die each year as a result of noncombat circumstances, including accidents during training.[38] C. J. Dick, an independent analyst of the Russian military, estimates that 1,000–1,500 conscripts die from *dyedovshchina* alone annually (Dick 1996, p. 5). Reports also show that at least 20 percent of soldiers leave the army "chronically ill" (p. 5). According to an Academy of Sciences report in 1994, a young man entering the army had an 80 percent chance of being beaten, and 30 percent of recruits will be beaten in a particularly savage way. Five percent will be raped (Waters 1996, p. 6).

There are clear antecedents in Soviet military culture and practice for the criminality and violence evident in the Russian armed forces today. Among these are:

- the theft of state property by all ranks in the army;
- *blat*, the use of official office for personal gain, is widespread in the Soviet and Russian bureaucracies;
- routine misuse of personnel, for example, to construct personal dachas for commanding officers;
- *yedinonachaliye*, or one-man command, understood as one-man authority. Military experts locate in this institutional rule-of-thumb widespread abuse of authority, including the countenancing of abuse of conscripts; and
- *dyedovshchina*, a particularly brutal form of hazing that acts as a system of control of conscripts. (Waters 1996, p. 6)

Lieven points out that hazing is not intended to break recruits down in order to build them up. It is intended to humiliate recruits in order to make them meek and subordinate. These practices are a central source of the devastating morale problem that exists within the armed forces today.[39] These antecedents have been transformed by the breakdown of the state. As Lieven (1998a, p. 292) argues, "The lack of [state authority leaves] only a veneer of autocratic but in fact largely powerless authority over a pit of chaos, corruption and a host of private tyrannies."

The problems evident in the armed forces are inextricably linked to the problems of society at large. This is apparent in the quality of the recruits entering the armed forces. In 1998, the army reported that one in three draftees was in poor health, one in ten was an alcoholic or had a serious drug addiction, and four in ten were raised in what the army described as "problem families."[40] Dick contends that a high percentage of recruits are characterized as in poor health because of the "bribability of doctors" and well-established techniques for faking illness. However, he maintains that recruits' physical condition reflects a real deterioration in Russia's public health in the 1990s (Dick 1996, p. 5). Dick points out that the high level of unfit and/or unwilling recruits represents another serious problem for the military: the declining prestige of the army and the desire of greater numbers of young men to avoid the draft altogether. Generous exemptions, especially on educational grounds, and the ability of the better-connected to avoid service have engendered a situation in which the ranks of the army are increasingly staffed by individuals from poorer families.[41] In other words, class has implications for one's exposure to the awful conditions in the armed forces. Widespread malnutrition, stories of vicious beatings, and the general lack of prestige now associated with military life have prompted growth in the number of people who try to dodge the draft.[42] The figure was about 23,000 in 1992 and has climbed to about 40,000 since 2000.[43]

According to Valentina Melnikova, press secretary of the Soldiers' Mothers Committee, the overwhelming majority of deserters from the army do so to avoid hazing. Although army officials consider this to be an exaggeration, they acknowledge that as many as 30 percent of soldiers flee because of hazing. In other words, they assume that thousands of deserters do so because of the extent of interpersonal violence within the armed forces.[44]

Deteriorating Army Conditions and Violence Among Russian Conscripts

Violence in the Russian military is an age-old and serious phenomenon. However, social deterioration since the early 1990s created a new set of conditions that makes life unbearable for some Russian recruits. In addition to the ever-present problem of *dyedovshchina*, malnutrition and general ill-health are much more serious problems today. As a result, chronic illness, suicide, the high rate of fatal accidents due to inattention, deteriorating equipment, and poor training techniques have conspired to make life in the army dangerous, if not fatal.[45] In addition, it appears that individuals from troubled social backgrounds and poverty are the candidates most likely to be forced into the armed forces.[46] The result is that as army life becomes more deadly, it becomes more and more the lot of the socially disadvantaged, whether for reasons of social background or physical and mental problems. The chief military procurator, Yury Dyomin, has characterized the situation in the following terms: "At the present time, given current funding . . . 'non-regulation treatment' stems in many ways from the poverty in all areas of our life. Many soldiers and sailors are half-starved and this gives rise to a whole system of extortion among them."[47] All these circumstances are pernicious in light of the fact that the conscripts are, of course, conscripted. They are legally bound to military service, which the Duma extended from eighteen months to two years in 1995 (Lieven 1998a, p. 215). For years, soldiers' advocates have pressed for a law that would facilitate alternative service. Alternative service is guaranteed by the constitution, but in practice it has been difficult for conscripts to qualify. A new law on alternative service, passed in 2002, was supposed to ameliorate this situation, but local draft boards have made it very difficult for young men who seek redress under it. Furthermore, Russia's alternative service is forty-two months, the longest such service in Europe, and conscripts can be compelled to carry out their terms thousands of miles from home on military bases where they may be subject to harassment by regular soldiers (Bivens 2003).

The procurement crisis in the military, the nonpayment of wages to officers and conscripts, the declining money available for adequate training, and lack of social support in general all make the Russian army incapable of putting an effective fighting force onto the battlefield. The result, especially when the political leadership is hopelessly corrupt and indifferent to the plight of its own army, is that eighteen-year-old boys possessing no training,[48] little to eat, and terrible morale are likely to serve as cannon fodder and to become brutally abusive themselves when actually called upon to fight a war. All of this has happened during both conflicts in Chechnya (see Chapter 5).[49]

Conclusion

In all the cases described in this chapter, individuals—whether children in orphanages, conscripts in the army, or people with dark skin who are refugees from other parts of the former Soviet Union—appear to suffer disproportionate levels of violence at the hands of state or state-sanctioned officials. Their constitutional protections are well specified. However, these protections are rendered meaningless by the realities of power that exist in the institutions and social contexts in which these individuals find themselves. Deteriorating economic conditions, and the social strife those have caused, exacerbate the violent climate and the latitude that authorities enjoy. In many cases, the perpetrators of violence, such as the Moscow police, are themselves responding to a breakdown in state functions that has denied them regular salaries. Given the choice of acting morally or of feeding one's family, the perversely obvious course of action is to reject common decency. The violence that accompanies much of this corruption may be no more than an attempt to justify the perverseness of the situation: if the victim of corruption is rendered subhuman, the act becomes easier to justify. Dehumanization and violence then become standard practice as a means to rationalize petty crimes. The outcome of such a fundamentally corrupt system is total impunity for officials and the violation of basic rights for disadvantaged people, including their right to bodily integrity.

Notes

1. The term "Caucasians" generally refers to people who come from the Caucasus region along Russia's southern border. These include immigrants

from Georgia and Armenia as well as internal migrants from Dagestan and Chechnya. For my purposes, the term is not necessarily meant to be geographically specific. Rather, it is to connote dark-skinned individuals, including immigrants from Central Asia, who are far more likely to be harassed by police than are fairer-skinned individuals. In fact, Africans living in Moscow and darker-skinned individuals more generally are subject to "racially" based mistreatment on a regular basis, for reasons I will explore in more depth below.

2. Reported by Agence France Presse, "Street Kid Numbers Soaring in Russia," December 16, 1998, from *JRL,* December 17, 1998.

3. This information was from a study ("Torture and Other Serious Crimes Committed in the Moscow Region") compiled by human rights activists in Russia, aided by the MacArthur Foundation. Its findings were reported by AFP, August 6, 2003, from *Johnson's Russia List (JRL)*, August 6, 2003.

4. The Russian term is *oligophrenia* and is very broadly applied to orphaned children.

5. According to MHG, human rights activists have repeatedly asked that independent observers be allowed to attend meetings of the psychological-medical-teacher's boards that perform the psychiatric evaluations but that such requests have been ignored (MHG 2001 report, p. 209).

6. The precise figures are malnutrition, 20 percent; rickets, 13 percent; anemia, 75 percent. From UNICEF's *Children at Risk* (1997), p. 83. According to data provided by Russia's deputy health minister, Olga Sharapova, only 30 percent of Russian infants can be considered healthy; disease among infants has increased 27 percent since 1997. "Thirty Percent of Russia's Infants Are Healthy," ITAR-TASS, July 11, 2002, from *JRL*, July 11, 2002.

7. As a general rule, the greater the degree of disability of children in a given institution, the more brutal and inhumane the conditions are likely to be.

8. Ukraine's economic crisis since independence has, if anything, been more severe than Russia's, and so the data just presented must be viewed cautiously. However, given important cultural similarities in the attitudes toward and treatment of disabled children, and the fact that both countries have experienced similar kinds of social pressures in the past few years, including growing poverty and declining mortality, the figure cited above gives some window on the magnitude of the problem in Russia.

9. MHG reports that, according to data released by the Procuracy, only 5 percent of those children are actually orphans.

10. It should be noted here that whereas HRW has been a consistent critic of economic reforms in Russia, the UN position has been much more supportive of the changes, regarding the development of private entrepreneurship and the breakdown of the central planning structures to be clearly positive developments. HRW does not oppose the market reforms in and of themselves. However, it does criticize their social consequences when it deems those consequences to have a directly negative impact on human rights.

11. For example, to correct cleft palate, which, if untreated, can have severe long-term consequences.

12. Figures cited in "Orphanages Violating Human Rights Routinely," *RFE/RL Newsline*, December 18, 1998.

13. Quoted in Celestine Bohlen, "Russia's Wards Survive on Strangers' Kindness and Native Ingenuity," *New York Times*, December 14, 1998.

14. MHG 2001 report, p. 205.

15. UN estimates place the total number of refugees at about 9 million. The figure represents one in thirty citizens of the former Soviet Union and includes at least 2 million individuals of Slavic ethnicity who lived outside their nominal republics during Soviet rule. Reported by Robert Evans, "UN Counts 9 Million Refugees in CIS States," *Moscow Times*, April 14, 1996.

16. MHG press conference, reported online at www.fednews.ru, January 30, 2003, from *JRL*, January 30, 2003.

17. See also John Daniszewski, "Racism Rears Up in Russia," *Los Angeles Times*, June 14, 2001, for a discussion of the increasing violent attacks perpetrated by Russian "skinheads" against Moscow residents with dark complexions. Daniszewski reports that police often will not undertake serious efforts to prevent or investigate such actions, even when such crimes are being carried out directly in front of them (from *JRL*, June 15, 2001). Recent legislation to combat extremism passed Russia's parliament and was signed into law by President Putin. However, critics contend that these laws are not adequately enforced and that in many regions local authorities, sympathetic to skinhead activities, choose to ignore complaints of beatings and other humiliations. "Russia's Culture of Racism," *Los Angeles Times*, July 19, 2002, from *JRL*, July 19, 2002.

18. The CIS consists of twelve of the fifteen former Soviet republics, excluding only the three Baltic republics—Estonia, Latvia, and Lithuania. According to the Bishkek Agreement, all member states of the CIS agree that "citizens of the Parties have the right to enter, leave and move about the territory of the Parties without visas, possessing documents certifying their identity or confirming their citizenship" (quoted in HRW 1995b, "Crime or Simply Punishment? Racist Attacks by Moscow Law Enforcement," p. 2, n. 4).

19. The financial crisis of August 1998 hit Moscow's economy especially hard, but the city is still relatively more economically vibrant than most other areas of the country. Goldman (2003, p. 15) estimates that 80 percent of the country's financial resources flow through it, and nearly 60 percent of direct foreign investment takes place in Moscow.

20. In 1995 the Russian government issued new guidelines under which localities could require visitor notification. In 1998 the Russian Constitutional Court struck down the 1995 law, saying that it violated the constitution's explicit provision of free movement and residence for all Russian citizens. The court ruled that notification requirements were acceptable but that local authorities were absolutely forbidden from restricting residency. Local authorities have, by and large, ignored the ruling. See "Court Strikes Down Some Residency Registration Rules," *RFE/RL Newsline*, February 6, 1998. A recent letter of complaint, sent by human rights activists to President Putin, notes that the *propiska* system had already been declared unconstitutional but was being used by local officials as a means of discriminating against certain groups of people, including Meskhetian, Kurds, and Armenians. Furthermore, legislation passed in 2002 has "exacerbated the possibility of applying citizenship legislation in a discriminatory way." The letter was publicized by Amnesty International, May 26, 2003, from *JRL*, May 26, 2003.

21. MHG notes that whereas Moscow's city police department asserts that

most crimes in Moscow are committed by non-Muscovites, data provided by the procuracy show that the overwhelming majority of perpetrators of solved crimes are, in fact, Muscovites (MHG 2001, p. 431).

22. The fact that there is substantial organized criminal activity in Chechnya itself, which among other things is said to control much of the drug trade in the former Soviet Union, was one major pretext for the Russian invasion of December 1994.

23. Gessen (1999) notes that numerous Chechens considered suspects in the bomb blasts, which took place in a central market in Moscow as well as in two apartment buildings, were being held for other reasons before the bombings occurred.

24. Whereas MHG regards this as "groundless," Mayor Luzhkov and others claim that Chechens were responsible for the 1999 bombings; I take no position here. My only point is that regardless of the degree of evidence, Chechens continue to provide a convenient scapegoat for Russian authorities intent on pursuing a variety of political and economic agendas.

25. Luzhkov has claimed that 40 percent of crime in Moscow is committed by "outsiders." Though he did not precisely define who fell into that category, it can be assumed that he had in mind Chechens, despite the fact that they are citizens of the Russian Federation, and refugees. Comment is from *Los Angeles Times*, June 1, 1996. According to the Moscow City procuracy, in 1996 those individuals classified as refugees committed 0.1 percent of all crimes reported in the city (figures cited in HRW 1997a, p. 6, n. 5).

26. This incident was reported in *Express-Chronika*, May 31, 1996. As of the report's publication date, the father and son had not yet been released.

27. As MHG notes, the 1993 constitution enshrines the right of free movement and free choice of domicile (pt. I, art. 27). Therefore, the Soviet-era residence permit system "ceased to be in accordance with the country's supreme law" (MHG 2001, p. 435).

28. Barry Renfrew, "Russia Tries to Save Its Military," Associated Press, July 2, 1999.

29. The assertion is based on David Fillipov's estimate that the U.S.$2 billion that Russia is thought to have spent on Chechnya in 2000 represents nearly one-third of the entire Russian defense budget. "Putin Now Mired in Chechnya," *Boston Globe*, June 21, 2001, from *JRL*, June 21, 2001.

30. "Defense Budget Not Fulfilled in 1997," *RFE/RL Newsline* 1, no. 194 (January 13, 1998).

31. "Russia's Military Spending to Soar by Nearly 50% in 2003," Interfax, August 16, 2002, from *JRL*, August 16, 2002.

32. For example, the draft budget for 2002 met with skepticism in Russia, because its assumptions were based on higher-than-expected growth and do not adequately account for a spate of debts to be paid off by the end of 2004. This is a problem for all government ministries, of course. In addition, it is apparent that the military officers are engaged in theft of supplies, including food, meant for beleaguered conscripts in Chechnya and elsewhere. Reported in "Doubts Expressed About 2002 Budget," *RFE/RL Newsline*, June 11, 2001.

33. "Russian Forces at 'Lowest Possible Level of Nutrition,'" *ITAR-TASS*, December 9, 1998.

34. See, for example, Carlotta Gall, "Deserter: 'We Were Like Animals,'" *Moscow Times*, May 14, 1996. Stories of soldiers deserting the army during both Chechen conflicts have been widespread, though the conditions are horrific enough to encourage significant desertions in peacetime as well.

35. Yuri Boldyrev, then-head of Russia's Audit Chamber, acknowledged in May 1996 that U.S.$2.5 billion had just been authorized for the war in Chechnya, but he could not say where the money was going or whether the allocation had really taken place. John Helmer, "Billions in War Funds Diverted," *Moscow Tribune*, April 1, 1996.

36. See, for example, "Latest Killing Spree Highlights Abuse in Military," *RFE/RL Newsline* 2, no. 18 (January 28, 1998).

37. The Russian defense ministry reported that there were 1,200 noncombat deaths through the end of August. Stephen Dalziel, "Death Rate High in Russian Army," BBC, September 14, 2003, from *JRL*, September 14, 2003.

38. Personal interview with Valentina Melnikova, press secretary for Soldiers' Mothers, June 25, 1996. Melnikova furnished data to me during an interview in Moscow in January 2002, indicating that 3,000 conscripts die each year. Gordon, in "Grunts of Grozny," reports that Russian soldiers regularly die in Chechnya at the hands of "friendly fire," a phenomenon so widespread that combatants have become resigned to it.

39. As I mentioned earlier, in connection with disciplinary practices in orphanages the term has a particularly violent connotation, which is why translations such as "hazing" misrepresent the practices being described.

40. "Military Finds Draftees in Poor Shape," *RFE/RL Newsline*, January 22, 1999.

41. Defense Minister Igor Sergeev noted in November 1997 that the "educational level of conscripts has fallen sharply over the past ten years." Reported in *RFE/RL Newsline* 1, no. 159 (November 13, 1997).

42. Anthony Clayton of the Conflict Studies Research Center points out that low morale, a growing aversion to military service, and the increasing ability of better-off youth to avoid the army were all characteristic of Soviet trends by the late 1980s. He notes that there was especially strong resistance among non-Russians, particularly from the Baltic states, as independence movements gained momentum. Additionally, vicious and sustained hazing prompted many recruits to try to avoid being called up. Clayton (1999, p. 1) notes that by 1989, 6.5 percent of recruits had criminal records, a sign of growing success in draft-dodging by socially better-off individuals. By contrast, in 1995 an estimated 15 percent of conscripts had a criminal record, which itself partly stems from the fact that juvenile crime in the Russian Federation increased by 76 percent between 1989 and 1995 (Waters 1996, p. 4).

43. See Dick 1996, p. 5; also see *RFE/RL Newsline*, January 22, 1999.

44. "Soldiers' Mothers Want Amnesty for Deserters," *RFE/RL Newsline* 2, no. 44 (March 5, 1998). The Russian constitution provides conscripts with the legal right to conscientious objection, under article 59, on religious and moral grounds in favor of "alternative service." In July 2002 legislation came into force providing for alternative service. However, the legislation was harshly criticized for requiring proof of pacifist credentials; acceptance of three years'

service instead of the normal two; and, frequently, that those performing alternative service live in the same barracks as soldiers. As a result, it seems clear that desertion will continue to be widespread in the armed forces. Fred Weir, "In Russia, an Army of Deserters," *Christian Science Monitor*, September 30, 2002, from *JRL*, September 30, 2002. The result is that the army continues to pursue conscientious objectors through legal channels. Lieven (1998a, p. 202) reports that although the army formally cites the majority of draft dodgers, it only charges perhaps 500, and only sixty get sentenced annually; in other words, the odds of successfully dodging the draft are high.

45. Lieutenant General Vladimir Kulakov, head of the administration of the army's general staff, reports that the rate of suicide per 100,000 Russian soldiers is now 2.5 times greater than it was for all Soviet soldiers in 1991. "Suicide Rate in Armed Forces More than Doubled," *RFE/RL Newsline*, June 11, 1997.

46. Twice-yearly drafts bring in an estimated 250,000 conscripts, but two-thirds get out of the army through student exemptions or for medical reasons. Weir, "In Russia, an Army of Deserters."

47. "A Division of Deserters Is on the Run," *Rossisskiye Vesti*, December 26, 1997, in *Current Digest of the Post-Soviet Press* 50, no. 1 (1998): 15.

48. The Russian army relies, to a substantial degree, on *kontraktniki*, paid soldiers who have already completed their military service and, often lacking better prospects, sign up for the much more generous rates of pay that the government has offered for service in Chechnya. The Russian army has relied more heavily on this group of soldiers during the second war in Chechnya than it did in the first; see Gordon (2000).

49. Among the more flagrant forms of corruption evident in the armed forces is the reported large-scale sale of plastic explosives and other weaponry by the 104th Guards Airborne Division to the Chechens in May 1995 while hostilities were in full swing between the two sides (Busza 2000, p. 123).

5

Institutional Degradation and the Two Wars in Chechnya

Focusing on Chechnya is necessary for several reasons. First, any study of human rights in post-Soviet Russia must acknowledge the extraordinary level of human rights violations that have taken place in Chechnya. Second, the conflicts there provide a good illustration of how a corrupt and weakened state, in the context of collapsing mechanisms of accountability, engenders circumstances in which human rights abuses may increase. Third, the war magnifies the degenerative factors in the armed forces that have facilitated ill-treatment of conscripts.[1] And fourth, the conflict has provided a partial justification for the ongoing mistreatment of darker-skinned individuals on Moscow's streets.[2] In other words, the conflicts in Chechnya, and the abuses they have spawned, are interrelated to the circumstances in which life-integrity violations take place.

Background

The Chechens' centuries-old conflict with Russia has been told many times elsewhere, and I will not recite that history here. Suffice it to say that the colonial wars of the past, plus the wholesale deportation of Chechens by Stalin after 1944, emerged as relevant grievances for Chechnya when Soviet authority began to fragment and split apart in 1990–1991. In the chaos of the breakup in the fall of 1991, nationalist forces proclaimed Chechnya to be a separate entity from Ingushetia, and on October 27, 1991, Dzhokar Dudaev, a former Soviet air force general, was elected the republic's president. A clumsy effort by Boris Yeltsin to introduce martial law in the republic only intensified Chechen desires for independence, and during the next two years Dudaev asserted strong presidential rule through what Anatoly Isaenko and Peter

Petschauer describe as an "ethnocentric regime" (2000, p. 7). In the fall of 1991, the pro-Dudaev parliament nationalized all enterprises in Chechen territory and stopped making tax payments to the Russian Federation.[3] Isaenko and Petschauer contend that a conflict emerged in Chechnya between a strong president and a resistant parliament that was strikingly similar to the one then unfolding in Russia, the latter of which was resolved when Yeltsin moved against the parliament in fall 1993.

The conflict between president and parliament in Chechnya revolved around many issues, but a critical one was the dispensation of land—particularly land that traversed key oil pipelines running through Chechnya—and who would control that dispensation. During this period, Isaenko and Petschauer note, pressure increased on the local ethnic Russian population: "together with the growing crime rate, the general instability and the rapidly worsening economic conditions, they fled the Republic in increasing numbers" (p. 9). In 1992 alone, nearly 60,000 out of more than 300,000 Russians living in Chechnya fled. Among other effects, the exodus of Russians depleted the educational establishment and industrial output in the region. Despite occasional setbacks in his confrontation with the more democratically inclined parliament in Chechnya, Dudayev received decisive support from oil-backed mafia interests in the region. Dudaev moved against opposition forces in June 1993, closing down opposition newspapers and storming the offices of democratic opponents, killing sixty people during one clash.

The developments in Russia and Chechnya—wherein presidents determined to resolve conflicts with other branches of government by force—undermined the emerging civil societies in the post-Soviet space and set an unwelcome precedent for the future resolution of conflicts. Many have contended that the events in Moscow in the fall of 1993 represented a fundamental break with the period of reform and openness that Gorbachev had initiated during the late 1980s. Most significant, it instilled in Russian elites the sense that they could resolve all conflicts by force. These developments, plus the evident breakdown in law and order in Chechnya, formed a powerful combination in spurring the Russian invasion of Chechnya in December 1994.

The First Invasion

In this section I highlight the scope of the violations of human rights committed during the conflict and place those violations in the context of the deterioration of the Russian state, as illustrated by events unfold-

ing from 1992 onward. Specifically, the loss of bureaucratic accountability for human life, in circumstances of endemic corruption and
intense social crisis, carried implications for human rights abuses by
government actors. For example, I return to Decree 1226, issued in June
1994, which allowed security forces to hold people without charge for
up to thirty days if they were suspected of involvement with organized
criminal groups. That decree abetted the impunity of law enforcement
officials to undertake sweeps of cities and towns throughout the country
and arrest, in large numbers, hapless citizens. They were caught in a
dragnet that was having little or no impact on the real target of the
decree: organized crime. Similarly, in light of Yeltsin's use of force
against the old parliament in 1993,[4] the decree that Yeltsin issued on
December 9, 1994, is instructive: "to use all means available to the state
to guarantee state security, lawfulness, rights and freedoms of citizens,
the guarding of public order, the fight against crime, the disarming of
all illegal formations" (quoted in Blinushov et al., 1996, p. 3). This
decree was issued just two days before forces of the MVD entered
Chechnya and the undeclared war began. In other words, the circumstances in which Russia's political leadership launched the war, and the
heavy reliance on MVD troops, increased the likelihood that the methods that characterized law enforcement generally would prevail.
Russia's military practices would include indiscriminate violence and
display an inability to execute military objectives, leading one observer
to note that the war "was from the beginning a war against the civilian
population rather than against military targets" (Cornell 1999, p. 86).
The war also was fought to the detriment of the conscripts themselves.

The Conduct of the War

When President Yeltsin ordered Russian troops into Chechnya in
December 1994, the Russian military leadership was confident of a
quick victory. Within a few weeks, it was obvious that the Russian army
had become hopelessly mired, with no easy solution. The Chechens primarily fought in small commando units. Their aim was to avoid major
detachments of the much larger Russian army and to engage smaller
units. The Russians, meanwhile, did everything in their power to avoid
direct combat with the well-trained and highly motivated Chechen
forces, unless Russia could assure itself of an overwhelming numerical
superiority in a given battle.

The Chechens, in this sense, did not constitute a regular army. They
moved in and out of civilian villages in search of favorable circumstances in which to pick off Russian detachments. One consequence of

this strategy, as well as of the fact that Chechen fighters received aid and comfort from local populations, was that the Russian army brought the war to civilian population centers. In direct confrontations, Chechen fighters invariably proved superior to Russian forces. The frustrations for a regular army (a poorly trained one at that) of fighting under these circumstances, in combination with the morale and material problems (see Chapter 4), had one crucial consequence for human rights: the Russian army carried out numerous atrocities against noncombatants.[5] This occurred in two forms: the use of aerial bombardment, the goal being "to kill and terrorize the civilian population"; and the "punishment" of local populations for separatist military successes (Lieven 1998a, p. 127). This form of collective punishment led to the destruction of many Chechen villages. It also led to perhaps the most notorious massacre of the first war in Chechnya.

Samashki and Other Atrocities

For the first three or four months of the war, despite Russia's claim that its goal was to disarm illegal formations in Chechnya and restore "constitutional order," its major military objective was to drive President Dzhokar Dudayev from the capital of Grozny. To this end, the Russian air force pounded the capital ceaselessly, causing thousands of civilian casualties, which included a large population of ethnic Russians. Dudayev's forces were driven out of Grozny in March 1995 (although they would later return), and at about that time the Russian army began to aggressively comb areas that were suspected rebel strongholds. Samashki, a town of about 15,000 civilians, mostly Chechen, when the conflict began, is in northwestern Chechnya. It sits on the Rostov-Baku Highway, a major thoroughfare that leads to Grozny. Chechen rebel units had been in Samashki, which was subjected to some shelling by Russian helicopters, but various observers say that villagers were unanimous in opposing the presence of rebel fighters in their village and that the rebels had quit the village in early March (Blinushov et al. 1996, p. 17).

Federal army officers continued to insist that Samashki was a Dudayev stronghold and that he had retreated there from Grozny. According to Human Rights Watch and the Russian human rights organization Memorial Human Rights Center (MHRC), both claims were unsubstantiated (HRW 1995a; Blinushov et al. 1996). On April 6, federal forces demanded that village elders hand over several hundred pieces of weaponry. The villagers said they did not have the weapons. A day later, Russian TV stations reported that Dudayev rebels had shot the village elders in Samashki, providing a pretext for troops from the

Ministry of Interior to take control of the village.[6] MHRC estimates that 130 people died during the operation. Sergei Kovalev, the human rights ombudsman for President Yeltsin at the time, put the figure at around 200 (Lieven 1998a, p. 133).

Although the operation at Samashki, which had the approval of the Russian high command,[7] was perhaps the most notorious, it followed a standard pattern of conduct by which Russian forces assaulted Chechen villages. The international watchdog group Médicins Sans Frontières described the typical procedure this way:[8]

- the issuing of a peace ultimatum, including the demand that villagers give up weapons and fighters;
- following an agreement between village elders and Russian forces, the Russians violate the agreement; villages continue to be bombed and villagers shot at;
- the village is required to pay the equivalent of several thousand dollars (an exorbitant sum) in order for the Russian army to open up a "humanitarian" corridor; typically, the corridor is not respected, and villagers are shot at;
- men and women are separated; males over twelve are arrested;
- villagers are used as human shields as Russian tanks enter villages; and
- looting is widespread.

In connection with these operations, the Russians established "filtration points" throughout Chechnya, which the Organization for Security and Cooperation in Europe (OSCE) estimated held several thousand prisoners in brutal conditions during the war, on the suspicion that such individuals were aiding Chechen commandos. The evidence suggests little, if anything, linking detainees to guerilla activity (Lieven 1998a, p. 133). There were also many disappearances of those taken to filtration camps. Anatole Lieven also notes that the checkpoints the Russian army established in Chechnya amounted to extortion rackets in which "the borderline between political detention and pure criminality becomes more and more blurred" (Lieven 1998a, p. 133). This was perhaps a predictable outcome given the chronic nonpayment of soldiers' regular wages.

Physical Decay and Moral Collapse

In August 1996 Chechen fighters reentered Grozny and routed the Russian army. This humiliating defeat provided the impetus for the peace agreement that Russian security chief Alexander Lebed signed with the Chechens in the fall of 1996. Chechnya's territorial status—at the heart of the military conflict—remains uncertain; the agreement only postponed resolution of that status for five years. Thus, without arguing the relative merits of the claims between Moscow and Grozny, I have tried to highlight some of the consequences of the lack of discipline and morale among the Russian armed forces. It seems clear that the Russian army brutalized civilian populations in inverse proportion to its ability to engage Chechen armed units. General Lebed, in the fall of 1996, estimated that 100,000 people, overwhelmingly noncombatants, died during the fighting. Lieven estimates a much lower figure of 20,000, in addition to several thousand Russian soldiers. This still represents an extraordinary level of killing in a population of about 1 million people (Lieven 1998a, p. 108). The conduct of the Russian military during the war exemplifies the degenerative features of life in the Russian army during the 1990s; these were bound to lead to disaster when poorly trained and ill-fed conscripts confronted a motivated and superior fighting force.

Additionally, the level of corruption among Russian elites and their lack of accountability for violations of law engendered a climate of impunity for forces operating in Chechnya. Lieven (1998a, p. 212) contends that "corruption [was] so all-pervasive that social and official (as opposed to personal) honesty [became] simply irrational, irrelevant, unpraised, and unrespected." This corruption is in turn attributable to deep changes in Russian society, which affected the morale of not only conscripts but all levels of society. Anna Politkovskaya, in writing about the second Russian invasion of Chechnya, elaborates on the depth of the corruption and its relationship to the misery inflicted upon ordinary citizens. She reports a booming business in illegal oil refineries in Chechnya; the loot is shepherded out of the country by Chechen mafia under the protection of Russian federal forces. Many of the armed skirmishes that took place in Chechnya resulted from conflicts among groups vying for control of local refineries. Politkovskaya also reported that local authorities who wanted to use the oil to rebuild the republic were wary of interceding in these skirmishes, or of calling to account those responsible for illegal activities, because the activities appeared to be sanctioned by authorities in the Moscow administration. "The crisis is intensified because not only has the economic chaos in the republic been artificially created, it is also energetically supported from Moscow" (Politkovskaya 2001, p. 228). The lack of any viable financial institutions in Chechnya opened the door for Moscow banks and other financial institutions to finance the millions of dollars in oil money pouring out of the region. This extraordinary corruption and cynicism appeared to have the most serious implications for the morale of Russian forces in Chechnya. Likewise, the extraordinary level of violence to which conscripts were subject every day, in the absence of any justifiable reason for that violence outside of the impunity of those who committed it, only engendered indiscriminate violence during the conduct of the war.

The Second Invasion

When the newly appointed prime minister, Vladimir Putin, assumed power in the summer of 1999, he vowed to deal with the threat of terrorism. In August, Russian forces moved into Dagestan, Chechnya's neighbor, to crush fundamentalist Islamic forces trying to wrest control from Moscow to establish an independent Islamic state in the Northern Caucasus. Then came a series of fateful bomb blasts in Moscow and Buinaksk that claimed hundreds of lives. The combination of these events, in addition to other political considerations, prompted the Russian invasion of Chechnya on October 1, 1999. Much as in the first war, the immediate pretext was to stamp out terrorists and bandits operating in Chechnya and other regions of the North Caucasus mountains.[9] As is well known, Putin's popularity surged, and popular support for the invasion was strong. Putin vowed to bring much greater firepower to bear this time to ensure a swift and decisive victory.

Russia deployed enormous firepower, including a relentless air campaign that devastated civilian areas, including the capital, Grozny. Putin also claimed early on, as he has repeatedly since becoming president on New Year's Eve 1999, that Russia was on the cusp of total victory. However, despite the early "successes," and despite the generally higher level of support for this invasion, the president's claims rang more hollow with each passing day.[10] In fact, in early 2004, more than four years into the second war, there appears to be no end in sight. Furthermore, the features that characterized Russia's conduct during the first war are also at work in the second war, including indiscriminate use of force, unchecked brutality against civilians, and the dismal morale among the Russian forces.[11]

Observers note that, as in the first war, the demoralization among Russian fighters directly contributed to reports of atrocities carried out by Russian soldiers.[12] Also as in the first war, many deaths in the Russian forces are attributable to friendly fire and *dedovshchina* (hazing), contributing to a high number of Russian casualties overall.[13] In addition, a persistent complaint during the first war was lack of training and experience. In the second war, "the soldiers were not the grizzled combat veterans the Kremlin insisted it was sending to the front. . . . They were untested conscripts" and became "little more than cannon fodder in Chechnya" (Gordon 2000).[14] Meanwhile, HRW (2001) reports that, in addition to the deaths of thousands of Chechen and Russian residents, more than a quarter of all civilians have been internally displaced; another 170,000 fled to neighboring Ingushetia. In sum, the second war in Chechnya, from the standpoint of human rights violations and senseless slaughter, appears to fully rival the first.[15]

One important difference is restricted media and scholarly access as a result of the Putin regime's intent to avoid the kind of reporting that undermined resolve during the first invasion. Journalists' access to Chechnya is much more restricted than during the first war; journalists are generally required to be accompanied by military escorts, according to Thomas de Waal, who covered the wars in Chechnya extensively. Also, media coverage of Chechen slave-trading and beheadings eroded whatever sympathy might have existed for Chechens' plight during the first invasion.

Journalist Maura Reynolds interviewed returning Russian soldiers; their stories support the claims of human rights groups that Russian abuses were widespread. Reynolds details how Russian conscripts carried out *zachistki* (cleansing operations) in Chechen villages. Conscripts openly described the methods of torture they used, falsifying accounts of supposed resistance, and their intention to kill, at the least, any fighting-age Chechen male. One conscript said, "They should get what they deserve. On one hand it looks like an atrocity, but on the other hand, it's easy to get used to." Common practices include a take-no-prisoners policy and the severing of ears as a ritual of vengeance. Reynolds invokes the notion of *bespredel* (chaos, without limits) to describe the situation in Chechnya. According to the soldiers she interviewed, a feeling that only Russians were being held to human rights standards and mutilations carried out by Chechens exacerbated their hatred of Chechens, which soldiers suggested was more intense in this conflict. Her interviewees also spoke of a "military culture that glorifies ardor in battle, portrays the enemy as non-human and has no effective system of accountability."[16]

Conduct of the Second War

As noted earlier, Putin sent a large invasion force into Chechnya for the second war and brought to bear overwhelming firepower. In contrast to the first invasion, this conflict was to be handled more by Kontraktniki (soldiers hired on a contract basis, as opposed to conscripted ones) and second-year conscripts, presumably better-trained and more experienced than the youngsters who bore the brunt of the fighting during the first war. Federal forces would be responsible for the military seizure of territory; special forces of the MVD, like the OMON, would be responsible for holding territory and pacifying it. The expectation with experienced professional soldiers was that Russian forces overall would be more efficient. Furthermore, the army offered material incentives to those willing to volunteer for duty in Chechnya. Contract soldiers and special police forces are paid the equivalent of U.S.$28 per day, compared to the $50 per month they would normally receive. But unchanged is the lack of central authority to impose uniform policies on soldiers for conduct during operations. As a result, if a commanding officer has the attitude that there is "no such thing as a Chechen civilian," then dire consequences will inevitably follow for Chechen civilians. And as the fearless Anna Politkovskaya repeatedly noted in her book-length account of the second invasion, there was no meaningful punishment for soldiers who committed atrocities against civilian populations. These include large-scale massacres, as at Aldy, a suburb of Grozny, in February 2000, when sixty-two people were killed. In June 2002, fifty bodies were found in a ditch near Chankala; corpses were missing eyes, ears, and genitals. Other mass graves have been found in Chechen Yurt, Argun, and Alkhan-Kala.

According to a joint report put out by the Society for Russian-Chechen Relations and HRW, in the one-month period between July 15 and August 15, 2003, fifty-nine civilians were shot dead, sixty-four were abducted, 168 were wounded, and 298 were tortured. Chechen men regularly disappear after being taken into custody by Russian soldiers or security police.[17] Anger, vengeance, and economic gain motivate much of the bad behavior in Chechnya. Kidnapped Chechens can be bought back by their families for several thousand dollars. The return of dead bodies, important for burial rituals, costs a little less.[18] In addition to the devastation and slaughter being wrought by the Russian army, there is a concern about serious, long-term consequences for those who fought in it. According to Aslambek Aslakhanov, who was Chechnya's elected representative to Russia's parliament and a supporter of the Russian incursion, a generation of violent and psychologically traumatized young men is returning home from the front.

Besides all the economic misery and physical destruction wrought by Russian forces in 1994–1996 critical to subsequent developments,

Lieven contends that new factors are important to recognize. These include:

- the failure of President Aslan Maskhadov and the Chechen authorities to create an effective state;
- the explosion of banditry and kidnapping as a major industry (estimates are that there were 1,100 kidnappings for ransom in Chechnya and neighboring republics between 1996 and 1999; many victims were tortured and mutilated); and
- the arrival and development of a "powerful group of international Islamic militants dedicated to carrying out the jihad against Russia beyond Chechnya's borders."[19]

Likewise, the respected Russian security correspondent Pavel Felgengauer reports that President Maskhadov now wears epaulets with Quranic verses on them, "a trademark of the religious extremist wing of the Chechen resistance."[20] Lieven does blame the 1994 invasion for the appearance of Wahhabism, the radical brand of Islam associated with Saudi Arabia, and Felgengauer blames Putin's refusal to negotiate with Maskhadov for his apparent turn since 2001 or so to radical Islamic elements, including, perhaps, Al-Qaida. Irrespective of debates about Maskhadov's suitability as a negotiating partner, it is clear that, since the siege of the Nord-Ost theater, the Russians have intensified operations in Chechnya. According to Sabrina Tavernise of the *New York Times*, in the two weeks following the end of that siege Russian forces cordoned off five Chechen municipalities looking for weapons and rebels, and several Chechen men may have been executed during the course of those operations.[21]

Conclusion

Whereas the first invasion and the overwhelming odds against which the Chechen rebels fought Russian forces engendered sympathy for the Chechen cause, the circumstances leading up to the second invasion, the international climate relating to the war on terrorism, and the utter breakdown of law and civility in Chechnya created a more complex situation the second time around. The notion that there are no "good guys" in this fight is widely held, and this appears to have made efforts to publicize atrocities in Chechnya more difficult or of less interest to ordinary Russians and the international community. However, little of substance has really changed from the first invasion from a human rights standpoint. The Russian army remains woefully undernourished and ill-equipped, and the leadership remains indifferent to the fate of its own soldiers, let alone civilians in Chechnya. This despite occasional admonitions by various members of Putin's government, including Vladimir Kalamanov, the Russian emissary for human rights and freedoms in Chechnya, regarding lawbreaking by Russian forces. The combination of pitiful resources, lack of accountability, and impunity for acts of violence mirror those in other realms of Russian life. In a September 2002 interview with Radio Free Europe/Radio Liberty, Andrei Babitskii, a journalist who was formerly imprisoned, rejected OSCE claims that the situation in Chechnya had improved due to ongoing efforts to build quasigovernmental structures there. Babitskii contended that the security of the civilian population has not improved at all. He further observed that

> every Russian person . . . more or less understands what's going on in Chechnya because the problems in the regions are quantitatively different but qualitatively the same. A person can be beaten half to death in a police station. That is, by essentially knowing the modus operandi of those working in law enforcement structures, almost every Russian can more or less exactly imagine, if not the details, then the character of what is going on there.[22]

Consequently, the issue is not who is responsible for the second outbreak of fighting, or whether Chechnya has been plagued by lawlessness and atrocities of its own doing. Rather, the issue is the scale of human rights violations of civilians and noncombatants, accompanied by the familiar problems of horrid conditions facing Russian conscripts. Sergei Kovalev also sees the second war as an outgrowth of a reaction of elites within Russian society against those who vigorously opposed the first conflict—the "vile liberals."[23] For Politkovskaya, the "moral" of so much of the corruption and venality in Chechnya is that "the State does not exist in Russia. . . . The Russian Federation is a case study in total and irreversible impotence. That vacated arena is now filled with the ambitions of some, and the laziness and indifference of others" (2001, p. 91).

This is not to allege any defect in the "Russian DNA."[24] Rather, I highlight a confluence of factors flowing from the circumstances of the Russian transition. A combination of declining state capacity, eroding accountability, a dearth of resources, and a general unraveling of any coherent political authority committed to protecting fundamental rights has meant dire consequences for some disadvantaged groups. These developments do not flow ineluctably from the deformities of Soviet communism (though, of course, those play a part) or from defects in the Russian character. Rather there has been a confluence of social, economic, and political forces that are not unique to Russia. The dynamics I trace here bear important similarities to those of other newly democratizing countries. In my view, that fact influences our understanding of democratization and the role that economic transformation plays in that process, especially as it impinges fundamental rights to bodily security.[25]

Notes

1. It is true that when then–Prime Minister Vladimir Putin initiated the second invasion in the fall of 1999, the Russian army brought greater firepower to bear than it had during the earlier conflict. As a result, the initial results appeared much more impressive, from the Russian standpoint, than had been the case during the first war. However, as the second occupation has dragged on for four-plus years, the problems that faced the armed forces in 1994–1996, including terrible morale, exceptionally poor training, and horrific abuses by Russian forces, have all resurfaced in a fashion strikingly similar to assessments of Yeltsin's war. There have been many accounts of the nature of the fighting there. See, for example, Michael Gordon, "The Grunts of Grozny," *New York Times Sunday Magazine*, February 22, 2000, accessed online from Lexis-Nexus.

2. The problem is not specific to Moscow. However, Moscow's relatively strong economy has made it a magnet for internal and external migrants, which in turn has engendered a particularly harsh response by the authorities to "illegal" settlers.

3. These moves were analogous to the actions taken by the Russian Federation against the Soviet Union, which assuredly accelerated the collapse of the latter.

4. Juviler (1998, esp. pp. 125–131) contends that the invasion of Chechnya was characteristic of the period 1993–1995, in which an authoritarian restoration of sorts was taking place in Russia. He contends that the 1996 elections represented new progress for Russian democracy. Sergei Kovalev, the human rights activist and former dissident, sees the attack on parliament (which he grudgingly supported) and the invasion of Chechnya as reflective of a new ethos among Russian elites, that of *derzhavnost*, which loosely translates as "stateness," but with strongly nationalistic and expansionist connotations (1996b, p. 10). Lieven (1998a, esp. chap. 4), by contrast, sees events in Chechnya as the ultimate extension of a particularly predatory form of liberal-capitalist ideology, one that cannibalizes state structures with the complicity of those charged with managing the state.

5. Cornell (1999, p. 88) contends that "Chechen fighters . . . continued entrenching themselves in villages which were subsequently attacked by Russian forces. Hence a certain blame must be put on the Chechen side for the

civilian casualties of the war." Cornell notes that the Chechens' use of human shields proved "useless" as a strategy, because "Russian attacks took place notwithstanding civilian casualties."

6. In May 1996, at a parliamentary commission hearing on the massacre, army officers acknowledged that the claims about Dudayev and the shooting of elders had been a lie. The commission did not ask them to explain why they lied or why, given that they now had no pretext for the assault, they entered Samashki anyway (Blinushov et al. 1996, p. 28).

7. This is according to the report produced by Memorial. Cornell says that the Samashki massacre was not sanctioned by army authorities but rather was carried out by rogue units. In his view, this "does not constitute an excuse, especially as neither the military leadership nor the civilian government has made serious efforts to investigate the event and punish the perpetrators" (2000, p. 91).

8. In Lieven 1998a, p. 131.

9. The scholar Robert Bruce Ware, an expert on Dagestan and the Northern Caucasus, has, in numerous postings on *Johnson's Russia List* (*JRL*), argued adamantly that the second invasion was fully justified by the serious threat that Islamic fundamentalism posed to the Caucasus region and that, furthermore, Dagestanis themselves overwhelmingly supported Russia's invasion on their behalf. Lieven (2000, p. 321) has contended that there are important differences between the first and second invasions because of the "attacks on and threats to Russia from Chechnya in the two years leading up to the war," and because of "the powerful forces in Chechnya and their international radical Muslim allies, who had publicly committed themselves to a jihad to drive Russia from the entire Northern Caucasus and establish an Islamic state." I do not weigh in on such issues here. From the standpoint of human rights, regardless of the justifications for war itself, the conduct of the Russian armed forces toward civilian populations in Chechnya has, by agreement of all observers, been indistinguishable from its conduct during the first invasion. That Chechens have also carried out regular atrocities is not in dispute here.

10. For example, Martin Sieff of United Press International reported in April 2001 that Putin had announced an imminent Russian withdrawal after the "pacification" of Chechnya. By mid-June, David Fillipov was reporting that the withdrawal had been halted after only 5,000 of the estimated 80,000 Russian troops had been pulled back and that many of those 5,000 were being returned to the front. Fillipov, "Putin Now Mired in Chechnya," *Boston Globe*, June 21, 2001, from *JRL*, June 21, 2001; Martin Sieff, "Analysis: Putin's Costly Chechnya Victory," United Press International, April 2, 2001, from *JRL*, April 3, 2001.

11. Francois Jean (2000), of Médicins sans Frontières, has noted that Russia, in addition to extensive use of bomber planes and heavy artillery used against civilian areas, has deployed surface-to-surface missiles in much greater numbers than during the first war.

12. Among the most notorious have been massacres of civilians in the village of Alkhan-Yurt and in the Grozny suburb of Aldi, where a total of seventy five people are believed to have been summarily executed. "Albright Urged to

Act on Atrocities in Chechnya," United Press International, March 23, 2000, accessed from Infotrac.

13. The Interfax news agency reports that 4,705 Russian soldiers and police officers have been killed in combat since October 1999. It also reports that 14,113 rebels have been killed during that time. Independent observers, like the Committee of Soldiers' Mothers, estimates casualty figures on the Russian side are perhaps twice as high and note that the government has become reticent about disclosing its casualty figures. "4,705 Russian Soldiers Reportedly Killed in Chechnya Since 1999," Associated Press, December 18, 2002, from *JRL*, December 19, 2002. In addition to warranted skepticism about Russia playing down its own body count, Gordon (2000) notes that soldiers who are wounded, but do not die until they reach a hospital, may be classified as having "perished as a result of trauma."

14. Though, as I describe below, there were more *kontraktniki* sent to Chechnya during the second war.

15. Maura Reynolds, "War Has No Rules for Russian Forces Fighting in Chechnya," *Los Angeles Times*, September 17, 2000, from *JRL*, September 17, 2000.

16. Ibid. One particularly notorious incident was the kidnapping and subsequent beheading by Chechen kidnappers of four British Telecom workers in 1998. Even Politkovskaya, a bitter critic of Russian atrocities and policy in Chechnya, cannot resist attacking human rights organizations for failing to face the monstrous nature of the crimes committed by Chechens before and during the second invasion (Politkovskaya 2001, passim).

17. Krystyna Kurvczab-Redlich, "Torture and Rape Stalk the Streets of Chechnya," *The Observer*, October 27, 2002, from *JRL*, October 27, 2002.

18. Reynolds, "War Has No Rules."

19. Lieven (1999, p. 722) has also noted that, before the first war, Dudayev's inability to control criminality in Chechnya was an important factor in prompting conflict, and that "any serious study of the Chechens simply has to pay attention to the way in which raiding (now transformed into various kinds of organized crime) and utter impatience of higher authority are deeply imbedded in their tradition."

20. Pavel Felgengauer, "Bloody Chechen Deadlock," *Moscow Times*, September 26, 2002, from *JRL*, September 26, 2002.

21. "Chechnya Is Caught in Grip of Russia's Antiterror Wrath," *New York Times*, November 12, 2002, available online at www.nytimes.com.

22. *Radio Free Europe/Radio Liberty Online Reports*, September 25, 2002, retrieved from *Johnson's Russia List* no. 6457, September 26, 2002.

23. Reuters, January 27, 2000, from *JRL*, January 27, 2000. Andrei Mironov, of Memorial Human Rights Center and a former political prisoner in the mid-1980s, similarly told me that the second war was a war against those elements of Russian society that opposed the first invasion and wanted to bring a greater consciousness of human rights to Russia. Personal interview, Moscow, January 14, 2002. The Russian political analyst Andrei Piontkovsky is one of many to describe the second invasion as one of "political opportunism." Before Chechen commandos seized 800 hostages in the Nord-Ost theater in Moscow

in late October 2002, there was growing sentiment for a negotiated solution to the conflict and public doubts about the nature and purpose of Putin's war aims. Gregory Feifer, "Chechnya: After Three Years of War, Support Rising for Negotiations," *RFE/RL Newsline*, September 26, 2002, from *JRL*, September 26, 2002. With the violent end to the hostage-taking, including the killing of almost all of the fifty or so commandos and another 120 civilians from gas poisoning, the calls for negotiation have lost what little momentum they had.

24. Lieven (2000) attacks what he calls the blatant anti-Russian chauvinism of many Western commentators. The "DNA" comment is from a column by George Will.

25. The international war on terrorism, whose rhetoric Putin has invoked in relation to Chechnya, only intensifies concerns that in addition to the structural and material concomitants of human rights violations, any political commitment to protecting human rights will give way to other priorities.

6

Russia in Comparative Perspective

In this study, I have examined human rights violations that are primarily a product not of a state's politically repressive apparatus but rather of socially vulnerable circumstances in a state that has undergone profound economic and political changes. Individuals may be victims of government agents, such as prisoners abused by prison guards; however, the notable fact is that, in all the cases I describe, citizens' rights to personal inviolability were compromised as a result of the failure of the Russian state to enforce its laws, leaving these people prey to capricious individuals or murderous social conditions. Therefore, the salient feature of the human rights violations I describe is a breakdown of accountability of state agents who are nominally bound to enforce existing law, which promises to protect individual life. Although such violations may seem less sinister in nature than those perpetrated by the KGB, the fact remains that large numbers of innocent citizens see their most fundamental rights violated.

Furthermore, it is arguable that threats to human rights that flow from state incapacity, prevalent in the democratizing world since about 1989, necessitate a reconceptualization of how we define human rights violations and the sources of those violations. Specifically, it is necessary to understand how component processes of reform can contribute to growing human rights violations, despite the presumptive improvement in human rights that formal democratization is supposed to entail. The point here is not to impugn democracy or democratization in the abstract. Rather, my intent is to raise questions about the form that attempted transitions to democracy can take under prevailing circumstances. Here, the Soviet legacy matters—but so, too, does the international context, as evidence from other protracted transitions suggests. In order to reorient our understanding of the potential sources of human rights violations, scholars must carefully scrutinize the circumstances

123

under which economic reforms and changing structures of authority can undermine, rather than promote, human rights.

Referring to Latin America, Guillermo O'Donnell has written that "there is a tendency when discussing democracy to talk in terms of nation-states as if they were cogent, unified entities. In fact, social relations within the political boundaries are highly differentiated and the presence of the state is very uneven" (1993, p. 50). O'Donnell delineates several zones within which different degrees of a state's functionality prevail. In his "blue" zones, "the rule of law is efficiently and equally applied across class and ethnic groups, and the bureaucracy is efficacious in administering policies across the entire territory" (p. 50). In a "green" zone, the state would be present throughout the territory of a given nation but weaker in terms of the "efficient and equal application of the rule of law" (p. 50). Finally, in the "brown" zone, the state's presence would be very low. For O'Donnell, the crucial question is why brown zones have been spreading in Latin America. He recognizes that in some states, like Argentina, persistent social and political crises have facilitated the spread of brown zones for some forty years. However, according to O'Donnell, the most salient cause of the pervasiveness of the "browning of Latin America" has been "neo-liberal policies—balanced budgets, tight money, privatization—[which] have been implemented across Latin America" (p. 51).

O'Donnell's map conceives of the state's reach in primarily geographical terms. Throughout this study, I have contended that the violation of people's rights is contingent more on their social location than their geographical location, though geographical federalism can have adverse implications for human rights, as is the case for dark-skinned residents of Moscow. In other words, I contend that federalism is an instance of a broader process of devolution of authority. Although democratization, by definition, extends the franchise and the formal realms in which citizens may participate and influence political decisionmaking, it does not necessarily extend the protections of political citizenship to elemental spheres of life, such as the right to personal inviolability. In my view, this failing raises the most fundamental questions about the perceived value of democratization and its current attendant form of economic reorganization: neoliberalism.

In turn, the component features of neoliberalism rest on a fundamental distrust and antipathy toward the state, as well as a fundamental belief in the market and private property. State planning and ownership are inimical to freedom; paring the state and its power is an unqualified good. For the architects of Russia's economic reforms, the massive Soviet economic planning bureaucracy stood as an insurmountable barrier to efficiency and adaptability in the late twentieth century and provided a clear rationale for attempting to cut the state down to size. Furthermore, the state's repressive apparatus was the only possible target of dissident intellectuals and "democrats" more generally. Therefore, the question is not whether the old Soviet state bureaucracy should have been left alone. Instead, the question is: In whose interests and for what purpose should the state have been reformed? The presumption was that neoliberal economic reforms, in conjunction with political democratization, would serve universal interests in the long term. The empirical reality is that socially vulnerable groups have seen their most basic interests—those in their physical persons—undermined by a particular kind of attack on the state.

Capitalism takes many forms, of course, and many capitalistic societies, especially in Northwestern Europe, accompany very high levels of social protection. What I describe here is not capitalism in the abstract but rather a specific variant of market-based reform that reformers attempted to implement in Russia. This variant, often referred to as the Washington Consensus, or neoliberalism, evinces characteristics evident throughout many of the newly democratizing states. These characteristics, including aggressive privatization, a reduction in social spending, and widening inequalities, appear to accompany human rights violations against the socially vulnerable in a number of countries other than Russia. This observation, meant only to be suggestive, nonetheless raises important normative questions about the form that transitions from authoritarian rule have taken since the early 1980s. In turn, it becomes critical to scrutinize carefully component features of economic reform as these features impinge upon individuals' life-integrity rights.

How, exactly, might neoliberal economic reform undermine the legal and institutional accountability necessary to protect people's life-integrity rights? Throughout this study, I have contended that there exists no single mechanism by which the erosion of horizontal accountability undermines life-integrity rights of individuals in different social-institutional spheres. However, I would contend that economic reform creates the context in which the various forms of unaccountability manifest themselves. In turn, a few key features of economic reform contribute to the circumstances in which some individuals feel impunity to violate the rights of citizens, as well as to the state's inability to ameliorate social circumstances that have fatal consequences for citizens trapped therein.

One feature of neoliberal economic reform that may, in a general sense, undermine accountability is what I would call its *ideological-discursive standpoint*. As John Dryzek argues, when individuals think in cost-benefit terms, and economic rationality becomes the arbiter for decisionmaking in increasing spheres of social life, their respect for the nonproperty rights of others may begin to dwindle (1996, pp. 92–93). Advocates of neoliberal economic reform do not openly endorse corruption and criminality. However, in keeping with the teleological bent of the supporters of neoliberal reform, corruption is viewed as functional to the agreed-upon endpoint of reform, which is prosperous, democratic capitalism. Referring to the phenomenally wealthy new oligarchy in Russia, Anatoly Chubais, the chief architect of Russia's privatization schemes, once said, "They steal and steal. They are stealing absolutely everything and it's impossible to stop them. But let them steal and take their property. They will then become owners and decent administrators of this property" (quoted in Lieven 1998b, p. 2). What is so insidious about this logic, as Anatole Lieven points out, is its effect on ordinary people. With such corruption and lawlessness so pervasive at the highest levels of government, to tell an ordinary Russian not to steal or, by extension, to commit other crimes "would be morally grotesque" (p. 2).

It is true that compromises made by Yeltsin reformers in the early 1990s, intended to mollify the so-called red directors, greatly corrupted what was, in any event, likely to be a chaotic privatization process. This fact raises questions as to whether it is fair to describe the economic reform in Russia as shock therapy or neoliberal reform more generally. However, from the standpoint of the discursive issues I raise here, it is clear that the Russian reformers continued to pursue far-reaching economic reform because of their desire to use privatization to bury the ghost of communism once and for all and because of the undeniable ideological legitimacy that such a course would confer upon the Yeltsin reforms in the eyes of major international financial institutions and the United States. Pursuing this course, and the political and ideological imperative of doing so, have the most serious consequences for ordinary Russians.[1] Russian reformers did not have to pursue the precise form of neoliberal reform that they did. However, their assumption of the broad mantle of "market reformers" ensured for them a level of latitude and support from key actors that helped the international community give limited attention to the more insidious consequences of the reforms. "Under the circumstances, Yeltsin's policies were the closest feasible approximation to Sachs' and the IMF's original intentions, and in this sense, the present perverted form of Russian robber baron 'capitalism' is the unavoidable product of the recipes purveyed by the shock therapists" (Reddaway and Glinski 2001, p. 235).

Aside from this general discursive problem, neoliberal reforms have tended to be associated with deep cuts in government-based social protection and other government spending, as well as substantial increases in income inequality and poverty that in turn drive growing numbers of people into desperate circumstances.[2] A specific feature of fiscal austerity, as is the case in Russia and Brazil, for example, is the weakening of precisely that institution most directly responsible for upholding the rule of law: the legal-judicial apparatus.[3] Moreover, as state institutions weaken in material terms due to budget-cutting, their authority erodes in moral terms: the corruption that appears pervasive among many new democracies undermines the moral authority of states to compel compliance with the law. These processes in turn contribute to a decline in horizontal accountability. As a result of the moral decline and the lack of accountability, agents bound in theory by progressive laws can flout the law with impunity. The consequence of such impunity is the growing violation of life-integrity rights of large numbers of Russian citizens.

In Chapter 1 (Introduction) I noted that some critics contend that Russia's uniqueness makes it an inapposite case for a comparative research agenda. Some contend that this is so for historical reasons, whereas others contend that the problem in Russia has been its failure to implement properly economic reforms. According to this line of thinking, the problems I associate with neoliberalism—which has been a constitutive feature of contemporary transitions from authoritarian rule—are rampant corruption, lawlessness, and the general failure to implement reform in Russia. In other words, I am merely demonstrating that some forms of lawlessness beget other forms of lawlessness. Furthermore, the corruption in Russia today is only a variant of the massive corruption endemic to the Soviet system, especially in its later years. Consequently, I am describing a process that, given the historical legacy of communism, is predictable and thus inconsequential for other states.

In response to the argument that Russia is a unique historical case, I contend that if life-integrity violations during the reform period were specific to Russia, then they would still be significant because so much of the democratization literature rests upon a conceptual worldview in which the totalitarian-authoritarian past was so completely unacceptable that any change must be good. However, as much research has shown, the growing scale of life-integrity violations today, and the processes that have contributed to them, are not unique to Russia. Ron Ahnen's 1999 study of the assassination of Brazil's street children details the growing violence committed by state or parastate agents in postauthoritarian Brazil. A 1998 HRW report highlights the extraordinary level of life-integrity violations in Brazil's prisons in terms eerily similar to those that I used in describing Russia's prisons. For example, "the chronic overcrowding that plagues Brazil's penitentiaries" has led the authorities there to use makeshift police "lockups" as holding cells. In turn, these lockups "are holding several times as many people as they were designed to hold." Furthermore, many inmates in these lockups, who should be transferred to other prisons or for court appearances after brief confinement, spend months and even years in detention (HRW 1998c, p. 1). As in Russia, overcrowding has contributed to rampant violence, disease, and death. HIV/AIDS and TB have reached epidemic proportions in Brazil's prisons, and qualified medical staff and necessary medicines are scarce. Although Brazil plans to build more facilities to alleviate the problem, observers believe that the response will be inadequate given the "continuous growth of the inmate population" (HRW 1998c, p. 2). The sharp growth in life-integrity violations in Brazil, as a result of the "disappearing of the state," is consistent with O'Donnell's classification of Brazil as "dominated by brown." The disappearance of that part of the state—the executive apparatus—capable of upholding the law and applying it equally to all citizens undermines Brazil's ability to protect its citizens' most fundamental rights.[4]

James Holston and Teresa Caldeira, also looking at Brazil, view the world's emerging democracies as "uncivil," in which "violence, injustice and impunity are norms" (1998, p. 263). Their specific concern is with police violence, and they show how the justice system is compromised in Brazil as a result of the harsh realities of economic reform, which has created growing inequality, increasing poverty and crime, and greater threats to personal security, with a concomitant explosion in vigilantism and what they call the "privatization of justice" (p. 283). Their study of the patterns of violence and social discord belie the presumption that "institutionalization of competitive politics will yield strong political parties and independent legislatures and therefore stable democracies in which the rule of law, access to justice and protection of civil rights are more or less automatic byproducts of formal regime change" (p. 287). So, too, is that presumption belied by events in post-Soviet Russia. Other scholars of Latin America have asked similar questions and found that the codification of democratic rights and the abstract theorizing about transition and consolidation do not address the real problems caused by maldistribution of resources and lack of accountability.[5] Brazil, like Russia, is clearly not a fully consolidated liberal democracy. However, Brazil has adopted key features of a democratic polity, including competitive multiparty elections, a raucous and contentious (if not always powerful) parliament, and a constitution that codifies a full range of internationally recognized human rights. Unfortunately, as in Russia, these changes have not resulted in better protection of life-integrity rights. In fact, the evidence suggests that life-integrity rights in Brazil have eroded for certain socially vulnerable groups.

Particularly disturbing about these developments, as O'Donnell contends, is that disjunctive features of new democracies may not be destabilizing or "incomplete" at all. Instead, such features may herald the emergence of a new, consolidated regime type, one with fully institutionalized, highly formalized elections and the informal (but no less permanent) institutionalization of "particularism" (1996, p. 35). O'Donnell defines "particularism," or "clientelism," as comprising "various sorts of non-universalistic relationships, ranging from hierarchical particularistic exchanges, patronage, nepotism and favors to actions that, under the formal rules of polyarchy, would be considered corrupt" (p. 40). Informal institutionalization seriously undermines accountability by destroying horizontal accountability, which would compel oversight of some state agencies by other state agencies. Particularism also undermines basic liberal freedoms, even when democratic freedoms, such as voting and the free expression of ideas, are intact. O'Donnell specifically notes that, in such an environment, the rights of battered women, the protection of domiciles in poor neighborhoods, and the right of the poor and other minorities to decent treatment are regularly denied (p. 45). He further contends that "somehow it was felt that this democracy would soon come to resemble the sort of democracy found in admired countries of the Northwest—admired for their long-enduring regimes and for their wealth, and because both things seemed to go together" (p. 46). In this view these regimes, although not necessarily sufficiently "democratic," are nonetheless stable regimes types, and in that sense they are, unfortunately, consolidated. O'Donnell concludes that democratization studies have been "swayed by the mood of the times . . . we believe that democracy, even in the rather modest guise of polyarchy, is vastly preferable to the assortment of authoritarian regimes that it has replaced" (p. 46).

Given these realities, it is important to avoid confusing the means (elections, formally democratic institutions) with the more basic ends of a secure, decent life, to which democratic institutions should contribute. The fact that life-integrity violations are so pervasive in Russia raises questions about the utility of the democratic institutions that have emerged there in securing these more basic purposes. As noted in the Introduction, this caveat holds irrespective of the recent erosion of even the more narrowly political rights under Vladimir Putin that seemed to be taking hold under Boris Yeltsin. Specifically, the focus on formal democratic procedures and nominally given rights ignores the critical problem of accountability, and this problem has been a pervasive feature of the entire post-Soviet period. I have shown throughout this study that a breakdown in accountability of actors in various contexts has negative implications for the protection of life-integrity rights. Importantly, the myriad contexts in which state agents and private actors abuse their power should also be viewed as a political problem, a product of indifference among political leadership to compel executive accountability throughout Russian institutions, from prisons, to the army, to law enforcement more generally.

Summary of Arguments

This discussion raises five important points. First, formal-institutional democratic changes do not guarantee that rights will be extended to the civil sphere. In many new polyarchies, political democratization has occurred alongside growing violations of people's most basic civil rights (what I call human rights), including the right to personal inviolability. Second, empirical investigation is necessary in order to demystify the teleological thrust of democratization studies, which simply assumes that the extension of one set of rights will eventually, if not immediately, secure other kinds of rights universally. Empirical studies must not assume that rights are improving but rather must ask which rights—for whom, and in what contexts—are better protected. Third, aspects of the reform process itself, especially the introduction of variants of neoliberal economic reforms, can influence negatively the protection of basic rights. It is important to consider carefully these policies in order to counteract the tendency to overemphasize prior authoritarian practices (and the people commonly associated with those practices) as primarily responsible for the setbacks or "incompleteness" of new democracies. Fourth, the focus on formal, universalistic aspects of democracies tends to ignore marginal, or socially vulnerable, population groups. However, this bias belies democracy's universal claims, because from the standpoint of democracy it would not be possible to justify the systematic violation of the rights of some groups of citizens. Fifth, democratization may accompany an erosion of accountability. A critical aspect of this is the growing weakness of the state apparatus that can facilitate the impunity of actors in positions of authority, whether in state institutions or nonstate spheres, with adverse consequences for the protection of individual rights.

It is not true that economic restructuring would negatively influence human rights equally in all times and places. Substantial economic restructuring in Poland and the Czech Republic have not prompted the severity of human rights abuses or social chaos more generally that are evident in Russia.[6] Furthermore, it remains to be seen whether Russia's economic growth since 1999 will begin to translate into improved social protection and, perhaps, increased accountability of the types I have described here. However, there is strong evidence that the situation is similar in form, if not degree, in much of East-Central Europe and the former Soviet Union. Roy Walmlsey, of the European Institute for the Prevention and Control of Crime, has prepared an exhaustive report on prison conditions in East-Central Europe and the former Soviet Union. Although Walmsley attributes many of postcommunism's problems to the "economic situation bequeathed by the totalitarian years" (1995, p. 6), he acknowledges that the political changes throughout the region in the late 1980s and early 1990s "introduced a range of factors that, in turn, led to a tremendous growth in crime" (p. 7). These factors included "removal of the main repressive features of a totalitarian regime, the opening of borders, social changes including a reduction in social controls, and the introduction of a market economy" (p. 7). This last factor affected crime rates both because of the "desire to 'get rich quick' . . . and [because of] increased unemployment with all the temptations that the associated poverty brings" (p. 7). As in Russia and Brazil, a consequence of the larger social processes has been the growth in prison populations throughout the former Soviet bloc. Between 1991 and 1994, the Czech Republic, Belarus, and Croatia saw a doubling of their prison populations (p. 8); Slovakia and Romania experienced 50 percent increases in their inmate populations. Despite some important variations among the countries under study, Walmsley (1995, p. 16) summarizes several characteristic problems common to all countries in the region. These include:

> the size of and continued increase in the numbers held in penal institutions;
> the conditions of pretrial detention, in particular overcrowding and the length of such detention;
> the limited resources available in present circumstances for improving the above conditions and for day-to-day running of the penal institutions;
> the shortage of noncustodial alternatives to imprisonment; and
> the prevalence of tuberculosis in penal institutions and the shortage of medical equipment and medicines with which to treat it.

A 1998 report on prison conditions in the former Soviet bloc points out that incarceration rates remain extremely high amid disturbing levels of violence, disease, and "profound human rights abuses" (Partridge 1998, p. 1). Furthermore, a 1998 report by HRW on police brutality in Argentina suggests that torture, murders of innocent victims during fabricated "shootouts," and deaths in police custody have been commonplace. HRW also noted that detention during document checks was common and that these and other "superfluous" detentions most commonly resulted in "torture or death while in police custody" (HRW 1998c, pp. 1–2). Nancy Scheper-Hughes's comparative study of the level of violence and mortality facing children in Brazil and South Africa points out that "decidedly lacking is any *intention* to rid the world of a specific class of people," specifically children (1996, p. 892 [emphasis in original]). And yet in both countries, following the onset of democratization, growing fear, crime, and poverty have created populations indifferent to the violent methods of both the state and private security forces in ridding the streets of such "dangerous" elements (p. 892).

Evidence also suggests that the difficulties facing women in Russia are not unique to women there. Here, certain aspects of liberalization, including the relaxation of travel restrictions, can have adverse consequences for women's life-integrity rights, when considered in conjunction with other social and economic factors. The Global Survival Network report documents the trade of tens of thousands of women from East-Central Europe and the former Soviet Union (excluding Russia) and notes, in all cases, the complicity of law enforcement and other government bureaucracies in facilitating such trade. Two other reports, by Human Rights Watch (1992, on women in Poland) and HRW and America's Watch (1991, on women in Brazil), suggest that the enactment of progressive laws concerning the treatment of women is not a deterrent to ongoing discrimination against women—in the workplace as well as in police response to violence against women—in the early years of democratization in both countries. Furthermore, recent attention to the sex-slave trade has focused on Moldova and the former Yugoslavia.

The above facts suggest that there is a global dimension to the phenomenon I describe. If this is the case, it becomes necessary to consider more global phenomena in understanding the causes of these life-integrity violations. This imperative is one reason that I have focused on neoliberal economic reform and on democratization's telos. Another reason is to emphasize the inextricability of discussing the rule of law from the resources—moral and material—necessary to uphold the rule of law.

In line with the arguments I have made, two possible future avenues for research are apparent. One would involve a more rigorously regional design, within Russia, whereby the variables I have outlined, including fiscal austerity, poverty and crime, and the resources available to law enforcement and other state institutions, could be tested against the propensity of regional authorities to uphold or ignore the law regarding rights to personal inviolability. One advantage of such an approach would be to identify more precisely the circumstances under which horizontal accountability breaks down to the detriment of human rights. Are there other factors, such as an active human rights community or a committed political leadership, that might mitigate some of the negative consequences of a dearth of material resources and compel greater accountability to the law?[7] Alternatively, it would be useful to utilize cross-national data, where possible, to test some of the hypotheses suggested throughout this study. Is there a relationship between income inequality and violence, and what is the social background of the likely victim of violence? What is the variation, in practice, of attempts at economic reform, and what implications, if any, does that have for variations in levels of human rights abuses?

As scholars have noted, globalization and neoliberal reform have come under growing scrutiny within academic circles and inside the corridors of international financial power. I have specifically tried to highlight the ways in which constitutive features of such reform have direct consequences for the violations of life-integrity rights. The scholarship's lack of recognition of the potential relationship is not a product of its active endorsement of neoliberal reforms. The omission is a product of certain teleological biases that engender an ideal-type in which all good things—prosperity, democracy, the rule of law—do go together at some point. As Lieven argues, this ideal-type is "culturally constrained and timebound . . . [to a] sanitised and homogenised version of the late twentieth century West" (1998a, p. 8). In fact, there are obstacles in the way of Russia's achieving a stable free-market democracy. However, many of those obstacles are not unique to Russia. They are present throughout the world and include "a weak state and legal order, a weak civil society, extreme and cynical individualism, corruption" (p. 9); arguably, these are characteristic of the form of democratic capitalism now predominant among the new polyarchies.

One implication of this argument is that economic processes are not as easily separable from political processes as scholars often assume.

Another implication is that teleological biases tend to distort our comprehension of complex social realities. The point is not that democratization itself causes the kinds of violations I describe. Instead, certain teleological assumptions make it easier to ignore the actuality of abuse of the socially vulnerable. The fact that Russia is the successor state to the Soviet Union only exacerbates this problem. Marginal population groups—to the extent that they are subsumed under categories of formal, universal citizenship—do not merit attention in most accounts of democratization, despite the fact that their experiences challenge the universal and positive claims of democratization studies for the citizens of democratizing countries. Finally, I contend that democratization studies rest too heavily on formal-institutional assessments of the requisites of functioning democracy based on an ideal-typical view of established democracies rather than a concrete understanding of the historical conditions under which institutional and societal features of life in the West came to be. What is called for, in my view, is more rigorously empirical work to assess whether reality in the new democracies bears out the claims that scholars make for democratization in the abstract.

On the eve of the 1996 presidential elections, two scholars of Russia wrote that despite "periodic reversals . . . all should understand that the command economy of Soviet times is dead and cannot be revived. . . . Russia is a pluralist society and will remain one. No Russian leader could reassemble the pieces of the old clock, and time moves in but one direction, even in the new Russia" (Stent and Shevtsova 1996, p. 109). The question is whether and for whom that fact, if it is true, is a cause for celebration. My intent in this study has been to compel the reader to attempt to answer that question while keeping in mind the right to personal inviolability that is presumed in our normative advancement of democracy.

Notes

1. Reddaway and Glinski (2001, p. 235) acknowledge the reformers' compromise with their putative ideological opponents by noting that "this is why shock therapy proved to be so lenient toward the old Soviet economic elite, while it was carried out with a remarkable consistency and obstinacy against the majority of ordinary Russians."

2. See Guillermo O'Donnell (1993), Thomas Callaghy (1997), and James Millar, quoted in Lieven (1998b). Writing about Latin America, O'Donnell contends that fiscal austerity has been particularly pernicious in this regard, in that it has "consigned great numbers of [citizens] to the ranks of misery without a social safety net of any consequence to cushion their fall" (p. 51). Thomas

Callaghy (1997, p. 394) contends that one effect of recent trends in the global economy has been the "emergence of an international underclass of weak states and economies that may be unable to benefit easily or quickly from economic reform and democratization." James Millar, the eminent scholar of Soviet economics, contends that "the default mode in today's world is not a market economy. It is stagnation, corruption and great inequalities of income" (quoted in Lieven 1998b, p. 1).

3. As Caldeira and Holston (1995) point out, the failure of democratization studies to analyze empirically judicial structures is noteworthy precisely because the rule of law and the branch of government most directly responsible for enforcing it would fit comfortably within a Schumpeterian notion of democracy.

4. Pinheiro (2000) documents in detail problems with the "(un)rule of law" in contemporary Brazil, including the extraordinary high kill rate by Brazilian police.

5. Elizabeth Jelin and Eric Hershberg (1996) call for an assessment of the relationship between broad macroprocesses of democratization and the measurable effects of these processes on ordinary citizens in Latin America. They ask (p. 1): "How does the process of regime change and its aftermath shape the life chances of individual citizens and social groups?" They note that issues of equity and social inequality became salient under the impact of adjustment programs that generally accompanied the newly liberalized regimes.

6. Although Poland is often held up as the model for successful shock therapy, there is substantial debate about whether Poland's strong economic performance is due to shock therapy or the substantial adjustments to shock therapy that were made after the first tumultuous period of reform. Marshall Goldman (1996, 2003), a noted scholar of Soviet-style economic systems, contends that Poland's success in privatization was due to its much more cautious and slow approach to the process than was the case in Russia. Grzegorz Kolodko (1998), Poland's former finance minister, contends that only when Poland substantially reintroduced a social safety net, and fundamentally altered the original shock-therapy course, did its economic performance improve.

7. This is the approach that Ahnen (1999) took in studying human rights violations in Brazil. He found that in regions with more active human rights advocates, other factors leading to human rights abuses were mitigated to a degree. In Russia, there have been a burgeoning number of human rights NGOs since the Soviet breakup, and the government has intermittently met with representatives of various organizations. Thus far, the impact on the scale of the abuses described here has not been noticeable in general.

Appendix: Interviews (all positions current at time of interview)

Lyudmila Alexeeva, member of the Moscow Helsinki Group; former dissident and political exile. May 30, 1996.

Boris Altshuler, chairman of the board, Moscow Center for Human Rights. May 12, 1996.

Vyacheslav Bakhmin, executive director, Open Society Institute–Moscow (Soros Foundation); former dissident and political prisoner. March 21, 1996, January 10, 2002.

Nina Belyaeva, president of Interlegal; legal consultant for nongovernmental organizations in Russia. April 25, 1996.

Valentin Gefter, Memorial Human Rights Center. March 11, 1996.

Boris Kagarlitsky, labor activist, author, former political prisoner. Numerous times between November 1995 and June 1996.

Mikhail Kukobaka, member of the Moscow Helsinki Group; former political prisoner. March 14, 1996

Marina Leborakina, independent feminist activist. June 24, 1996.

Tanya Lokshina, director of international programs, Moscow Helsinki Group. January 14, 2002.

Valentina Melnikova, press secretary, Soldiers' Mothers Committee. May 31, 1996, January 17, 2002.

Alexander Mironenko, director, Institute for Penitentiary Reform. June 13, 1996.

Andrei Mironov, member of Memorial Human Rights Center. January 14, 2002.

Victor Orekhov, human rights activist; former KGB captain and political prisoner. July 1, 1996.

Alexander Podrabinek, editor in chief, *Express-Chronika*, a human rights newspaper; former dissident and political prisoner. June 5, 1996.

Lev Ponomarev, member of the Moscow Helsinki Group; former member of Democratic Russia and the Russian Supreme Soviet. June 18, 1996.

Anatoly Pristavkhin, head of the state Pardons Commission. June 20, 1996.

Yuri Samodurov, director, Sakharov Museum and Public Center. January 16, 2002.

Valery Sergeev, deputy director, Moscow Center for Prison Reform. March 14, 1996.

Victoria Sergeeva, Penal Reform International, January 17, 2002.

Alexei Simonov, director, Glasnost Defense Foundation for the protection of journalists. May 20, 1996.

Alexei Smirnov, director, Moscow Center for Human Rights; former political prisoner. February 1, 1996.

Irene Stevenson, Moscow director of Free Trade Union Institute. Several interviews between March and June 1996.

Martina Vandenburg, head of the Women's Consortium. February 9, 1996.

Acronyms and Abbreviations

AI	Amnesty International
CEDAW	Convention for the Elimination of All Forms of Discrimination Against Women
CIS	Commonwealth of Independent States
CPSU	Communist Party of the Soviet Union
GDP	gross domestic product
GSN	Global Survival Network
HRW	Human Rights Watch
ICCPR	International Covenant on Civil and Political Rights
IMF	International Monetary Fund
MCPR	Moscow Center for Prison Reform
MHG	Moscow Helsinki Group
MHRC	Memorial Human Rights Center
MMS	Moscow Migration Service
MVD	Ministry of Internal Affairs
NEP	New Economic Policy
OSCE	Organization for Security and Cooperation in Europe
PTS	Political Terror Scale
RAN	Russian Academy of Sciences
SIZO	pretrial detention center
TB	tuberculosis
UDHR	Universal Declaration of Human Rights
UN	United Nations

Bibliography

Abramkin, Valery. 1996a. "On the Concept of the Reform of the Russian Penal System." Trans. Valery Sergeev. Moscow: Moscow Center for Prison Reform.

———. 1996b. "When the Fountain Is Playing . . ." (in Russian). From a presentation to a parliamentary hearing on the proposed Criminal Code of the Russian Federation, October 24, 1995.

"Against an Unjust Sentence" (in Russian). 1996. *Express-Chronika*, June 14, p. 4.

Ahnen, Ron. 1999. "Defending Human Rights Under Democracy: The Case of Minors in Brazil." Unpublished diss. University of North Carolina–Chapel Hill.

"Albright Urged to Act on Atrocities in Chechnya." 2000. United Press International, March 23. Accessed from Infotrac database.

Alexeeva, Lyudmila. 1984. *History of Dissent in the USSR: A New Period*. Benson, VT: Khronika.

———. 1990. *The Thaw Generation: Coming of Age in the Post-Stalin Era*. Boston: Little Brown.

Americas Watch. 1991. *Criminal Injustice: Violence Against Women in Brazil*. New York: Human Rights Watch.

Amnesty International. 1984–1995. *The Amnesty International Report*. London: Amnesty International.

———. 1996. "Urgent Action Appeal: Ethnic Chechens in Moscow." July 22.

———. 1997. "Torture in Russia: 'This Man-Made Hell.'" Available online at www.amnesty.org/ailib/aipub/1997/EUR/44600497.htm. Accessed on July 8, 1998.

Anderson, Lisa. 1997. "Introduction/Transitions to Democracy: A Special Issue in Memory of Dankwart Rustow." *Comparative Politics* 29(3): 253–261.

Applebaum, Anne. 2003. *Gulag: A History*. New York: Doubleday.

Arat, Zehra. 1988. "Can Democracy Survive Where There Is a Gap Between Political and Economic Rights?" In David Cingranelli, ed., *Human Rights Theory and Measurement* (hereafter *Human Rights Theory*). New York: St. Martin's, pp. 221–235.

Arbatov, Alexei. 1998. "Military Reform in Russia: Dilemmas, Obstacles, and Prospects." *International Security* 22(4): 83–134.

Ardashvilli, Alexander. 1996. "Before the Fall: Economic and Social Problems." In Wilma Rule and Norma C. Noonan, eds., *Russian Women in Politics and Society* (hereafter *Politics and Society*). Westport, CT: Greenwood, pp. 97–107.

Ashwin, Sarah, and Elain Bowers. 1997. "Do Russian Women Want to Work?" In Mary Buckley, ed., *Post-Soviet Women: From the Baltic to Central Asia* (hereafter *Post-Soviet Women*). Cambridge: Cambridge University Press, pp. 21–37.

Aslund, Anders. 1995. *How Russia Became a Market Economy*. Washington, D.C.: Brookings Institution.

———. 1997. "Social Problems and Policy in Post-Communist Russia." In Ethan Kapstein and Michael Mandlebaum, eds., *Sustaining the Transition: The Social Safety Net in Post-Communist Europe*. New York: Council on Foreign Relations, pp. 124–146.

———. 2001. "Russia." *Foreign Policy* 125 (July–August): 200–225.

Atkinson, Dorothy, Alexander Dallin, and Gail Warshofsky Lapidus. 1977. *Women in Russia* (hereafter *Women in Russia*). Stanford: Stanford University Press.

Attwood, Lynne. 1996. "The Post-Soviet Woman in the Move to the Market: A Return to Domesticity and Dependence?" In Rosalind Marsh, ed., *Women in Russia and Ukraine* (hereafter *Russia and Ukraine*). Cambridge: Cambridge University Press, pp. 255–266.

———. 1997. "She Was Asking for It: Rape and Domestic Violence Against Women." In *Post-Soviet Women*, pp. 99–118.

Bakatin, Vadim. 1995. "Commentary Views Criminal Statistics for 1994." *Moskovskaya Pravda*, May 18. From Foreign Broadcast Information Service (FBIS), SOV-095–96 S, pp. 26–28.

Bales, Kevin. 1999. *Disposable People: New Slavery in the Global Economy.* Berkeley: University of California Press.

Barber, Benjamin. 1995. *Jihad vs. McWorld*. New York: Times Books.

Bennett, Vanora. 1997. "Russia's Ugly Little Secret: Misogyny." *Los Angeles Times*, December 6, pp. 1, 8.

Bivens, Matt. 2003. "A Glum Report Card on Russia." *Moscow Times*, June 2. From *Johnson's Russia List* (a daily e-mail newsletter with information and analysis about contemporary Russia from a wide range of sources), June 2.

Blasi, Joseph, Maya Kroumova, and Douglas Kruse. 1997. *Kremlin Capitalism: The Privatization of the Russian Economy*. Ithaca, NY: ILR Press.

Blinushov, A., et al. 1996. "By All Available Means: The Russian Federation Ministry of Internal Affairs Operation in the Village of Samashki: April 7–8, 1995." Trans. Rachel Denber. Moscow: Memorial Human Rights Center.

Bohlen, Celestine. 1998. "In the Ruble Crisis, Even Prisoners Go Hungry." *New York Times*, December 14, p. A3.

Bollen, Kenneth. 1983. "World System Position, Dependency, and Democracy: Further Issues in the Measurement and Effects of Political Democracy." *American Sociological Review* 48(4): 468–479.

———. 1991. "Political Democracy: Conceptual and Measurement Traps." In Alex Inkeles, ed., *On Measuring Democracy* (hereafter *On Measuring Democracy*). New Brunswick, NJ: Transaction, pp. 3–20.

Borogan, Irina, and Grigory Savint. 1998. "The Girls from Tver Street in the Arms of the Law." *Sevodnya*, February 4, p. 7. In *Current Digest of the Post-Soviet Press* 50(5): 16–27.

Boudreaux, Richard. 1996. "The Man Who Rules Moscow." *Los Angeles Times*, June 1, pp. A1, A14.

Bridger, Susan. 1996. *No More Heroines: Russian Women and the Market*. New York: Routledge.

Brown, Archie. 1996. *The Gorbachev Factor*. Oxford: Oxford University Press.

Buckley, Mary. 1989. *Women and Ideology in the Soviet Union*. Ann Arbor: University of Michigan Press.

Bunce, Valerie. 1995. "Should Transitologists Be Grounded?" *Slavic Review* 54(1): 111–127.

———. 1999. "The Political Economy of Post-Socialism." Draft of article forthcoming in *Slavic Review*, presented to the University Center for International Studies, Chapel Hill, North Carolina, April 1999.

Bunch, Charlotte. 1990. "Women's Rights as Human Rights: Toward a Re-Vision of Human Rights." *Human Rights Quarterly* 12(4): 486–498.

Burkhart, Ross E., and Michael S. Lewis-Beck. 1994. "Comparative Democracy: The Economic Development Thesis." *American Political Science Review* 88(4): 903–910.

Busza, Eva. 2000. "State Dysfunctionality, Institutional Decay, and the Russian Military." In Valerie Sperling, ed., *Building the Russian State* (hereafter *Building the Russian State*). Boulder: Westview, pp. 113–136.

Caldeira, Teresa. 1996. "Crime and Individual Rights: Reframing the Question of Violence in Latin America." In Elizabeth Jelin and Eric Hershberg, eds., *Constructing Democracies* (hereafter *Constructing Democracies*). Boulder: Westview, pp. 197–211.

Caldeira, Teresa P. R., and James Holston. 1995. "Citizenship, Justice, Law: Limits and Prospects of Democratization in Brazil." Paper prepared for the North-South Center of Miami, Florida.

Caldwell, Gillian, Steven Galster, and Nadia Stenzer. 1997. "Crime and Servitude: An Expose of the Traffic in Women for Prostitution from the Newly Independent States." Paper presented at the conference "The Trafficking of NIS Women Abroad," Moscow, November 3–5. From *Global Survival Network*, available online at www.globalsurvival. net/femaletrade/9711russia.html. Accessed April 9, 1998.

Callaghy, Thomas. 1997. "Globalization and Marginalization: Debt and the International Underclass." *Current History* 96(613): 392–396.

Carleton, David, and Michael Stohl. 1985. "The Foreign Policy of Human Rights: Rhetoric and Reality from Jimmy Carter to Ronald Reagan." *Human Rights Quarterly* 7(2): 205–229.

Chalidze, Valery. 1977. *Criminal Russia: Essays on Crime in the Soviet Union*. Trans. P. S. Falla. New York: Random House.

Clarke, Simon, and Pavel Burawoy. 1993. *What About the Workers? Workers and the Transition to Capitalism in Russia*. London: Verso.

Clayton, Anthony. 1999. "Ethnicity and Nationalism in the Soviet Army, 1979–1991." Paper presented at the ninth annual conference of the Association for the Study of Ethnicity and Nationalism, London School of Economics, March 25–26. London: Conflict Studies Research Center.

Cohen, Stephen F. 1999. "Russian Studies Without Russia." *Post-Soviet Affairs* 15(1): 37–55.

Collier, David, and Steven Levitsky. 1996. "Democracy with Adjectives: Conceptual Innovation in Comparative Research." Working paper for the Kellogg Institute for International Studies, University of Notre Dame.

Connor, Walter. 1972. *Deviance in Soviet Society: Crime, Delinquency, and Alcoholism.* New York: Columbia University Press.

"Consideration of Reports Submitted by States Parties Under Article 40 of the Covenant." 1995. Comments of the United Nations Committee on Human Rights in Consideration of the Fourth Periodic Report of the Russian Federation in compliance with the International Covenant on Civil and Political Rights (ICCPR), at the Fifty-Fourth Session of the Human Rights Committee, July 17–18. M/CCPR/C/54/CMT/RUS/3.

"Consideration of Reports Submitted by States Parties Under Article 44 of the Covenant." 1997. Comments of the United Nations Committee on Human Rights in Consideration of Russia's compliance with the Convention on the Rights of the Child. Considered for Review, November 26, 1998. CRC/C/65/Add.5 (State Party Report). Available online at www.unhchr.ch/tbs/doc.nsf/MasterFrameView/d71205c3fb8645f8025670d0053ef48?Opendocument. Accessed June 1, 1999.

"Constitution of the Russian Federation." 1994. Trans. Federal News Service. Washington, D.C.

Cook, Rebecca. 1993. "Women's International Human Rights: The Way Forward." *Human Rights Quarterly* 15(2): 230–261.

Cornell, Svante. 1999. "International Reactions to Massive Human Rights Violations: The Case of Chechnya." *Europe-Asia Studies* 51(1): 85–100.

Country Reports. 1996. "Russian Human Rights Practices, 1995." Washington, D.C.: Government Printing Office.

———. 1998. "Russia Country Report on Human Rights Practices for 1997." Washington, D.C.: Government Printing Office. Available online at www.state.gov/www/global/human_rights/1997_hrp_report/russia.html. Accessed on May 4, 1998.

Cranston, Maurice. 1979. "What Are Human Rights?" In Walter Laqueur and Barry Rubin, eds., *The Human Rights Reader* (hereafter *Human Rights Reader*). Philadelphia: Temple University Press, pp. 17–25.

Dahl, Robert. 1971. *Polyarchy: Participation and Opposition.* New Haven, CT: Yale University Press.

———. 1998. On Democracy. New Haven, CT: Yale University Press.

Daniszewski, John. 2001. "Racism Rears Up in Russia," *Los Angeles Times*, June 14, 2001. From *Johnson's Russia List*, June 15, 2001.

Davenport, Christian. 1996. "The Weight of the Past: Exploring Lagged Determinants of Political Repression." *Political Research Quarterly* 49(2): 377–405.

DeBardeleben, Joan. 1997. *Russian Politics in Transition*. 2nd ed. Boston: Houghton-Mifflin.

Deloach, Stephen, and Annie Hoffman. 2002. "Russia's Second Shift: Is Housework Hurting Women's Wages?" *Atlantic Economic Journal* 30(4): 422–432.

Desai, Padma, and Todd Idson. 2000. *Work Without Wages: Russia's Nonpayment Crisis*. Cambridge: MIT Press.

Diamond, Larry. 1996. "Is the Third Wave Over?" *Journal of Democracy* 7(3): 20–37.

Dick, C. J. 1996. "A Bear Without Claws: The Russian Army in the Nineties." London: Conflict Studies Research Centre.

Doder, Dusko, and Louise Branson. 1990. *Heretic in the Kremlin*. New York: Viking.

Donnelly, Jack. 1989. *Universal Human Rights in Theory and Practice*. Ithaca, NY: Cornell University Press.

———. 1993. *International Human Rights*. Boulder: Westview.

———. 1999. "Human Rights, Democracy and Development." Paper presented to the University Center for International Studies, University of North Carolina, Chapel Hill, February 1999.

Dryzek, John. 1996. *Democracy in Capitalist Times: Ideas, Limits, and Struggles*. Oxford: Oxford University Press.

Ekiert, Grzegorz. 1991. "Democratization Processes in East Central Europe." *British Journal of Political Science* 21(3): 285–313.

Engel, Barbara. 1987. "Women in Russia and the Soviet Union." *Signs* 12(4): 781–796.

Evangelista, Matthew. 2002. *The Chechen Wars: Will Russia Go the Way of the Soviet Union?* Washington, D.C.: Brookings Institution.

Farnsworth, Beatrice Brodsky. 1977. "Bolshevik Alternatives and the Soviet Family: The 1926 Marriage Law Debate." In *Women in Russia*, pp. 139–165.

Fein, Helen. 1995. "More Murder in the Middle: Life-Integrity Violations and Democracy in the World, 1987." *Human Rights Quarterly* 17(1): 170–191.

Felgengauer, Pavel. 2002. "Bloody Chechen Deadlock." *Moscow Times*, September 26. From *Johnson's Russia List*, September 26, 2002.

Fillipov, David. 2001. "Putin Now Mired in Chechnya," *Boston Globe*, June 21, 2001. From *Johnson's Russia List*, June 21, 2001.

Filtzer, Donald. 1996. "Industrial Working Conditions and the Political Economy of Female Labour During Perestroika." In *Russia and Ukraine*, pp. 214–227.

Fischer, Mary Ellen, ed. 1996. *Establishing Democracies* (hereafter *Establishing Democracies*). Boulder: Westview.

Fish, M. Steven. 1995. *Democracy from Scratch: Opposition and Regime in the New Russian Revolution*. Princeton, NJ: Princeton University Press.

———. 1998. "The Determinants of Economic Reform in the Post-Communist World." *East European Politics and Society* 12(1): 31–78.

Fitzpatrick, Catherine. 2003. "Monitors Issue Unprecedented Prison Report." RFE/RL *(Un)Civil Societies* 4(14). From *Johnson's Russia List*, June 9, 2003.

Fogelsong, Todd. 1996. "The Reform of Criminal Justice and Evolution of Judicial Dependence in Late Soviet Russia." In Peter Solomon, ed., *Reforming Justice in Russia, 1864–1996* (hereafter *Reforming Justice*). New York: M. E. Sharpe, pp. 282–324.

Freedom House. 1989, 1990, 1991, 1992, 1994. *Freedom in the World: Political Rights and Civil Liberties*. New York: Freedom House.

Friedman, Benjamin. 1999. "The Power of the Electronic Herd." *New York Review of Books* 46(12): 40–44.

Friedrich, Carl J., and Zbigniew Brzezinski. 1956. *Totalitarian Dictatorship and Autocracy*. Cambridge: Harvard University Press.

Gaddy, Clifford, and Barry Ickes. 1998. "Russia's Virtual Economy." *Foreign Affairs* 77(5): 53–67.

Gall, Carlotta. 1996. "Deserter: 'We Were Like Animals.'" *Moscow Times*, May 14, p. 4.

Gessen, Masha. 1996. "Without Complexes" (in Russian). *Itogi* 29.

———. 1999. "Moscow Dispatch: The Clampdown." *New Republic*, October 4, pp. 18–21.

Gilinski, Yakov. 1993. "Penitentiary Policy in Russia." In *Prison Reform in the Former Totalitarian States: Issue 2*, pp. 37–39.

Gills, Barry, Joel Rocamora, and Richard Wilson, eds. 1993. *Low Intensity Democracy: Political Power in the New World Order*. London: Pluto Press with the Transnational Institute.

Gleason, Abbott. 1995. *Totalitarianism: The Inner Origins of the Cold War*. Oxford: Oxford University Press.

Goldgeier, James, and Michael McFaul. 2003. "'New Russia Ailing'; Stand Up, Mr. Bush: Putin Is Presiding over a Steady Erosion of Rights and Freedoms." *Los Angeles Times*, September 21. From *Johnson's Russia List*, September 21, 2003.

Goldman, Marshall. 1996. *Lost Opportunity: What Has Made Economic Reform in Russia So Difficult?* New York: W. W. Norton.

———. 2003. *The Piratization of Russia: Russian Reform Goes Awry*. New York: Routledge.

Golovachov, Vitaly. 1996. "'I Don't Deny Myself Anything,' Six Million Russians Citizens Can Say Today. 'I'm Poor,' 40 Million Fellow Citizens Will Reply." *Trud*, October 10, pp. 1, 4. In *Current Digest of the Post-Soviet Press* 48(44): 16–17.

Gomez, Mario. 1995. "Social Economic Rights and Human Rights Commissions." *Human Rights Quarterly* 17(1): 155–169.

Gondolf, Edward, and Dmitri Shestakov. 1997. "Spousal Homicide in Russia Versus the United States: Preliminary Findings and Implications." *Journal of Family Violence* 12(1): 63–74.

Goorha, Prateek. 2001. "The Political Economy of Federalism in Russia." *Demokratizatsiya* 9(1). Accessed from Infotrac database.

Gordeyev, Alexander. 1994. "Vague Prison Laws Fuel Inmate Abuse." *Moscow Times*, July 22, p. 4.

Gordon, Michael. 2000. "The Grunts of Grozny." *New York Times Sunday Magazine*, February 22. Accessed from Lexis-Nexus.

Goskomstat. 1996, 1997. *Russian Statistical Yearbook* (in Russian). Moscow: Goskomstat.

———. (In Russian and English.) 2003. Accessed from Russian/CIS Statistical Publications, UNC Chapel Hill online database collection.

Graham, Thomas. 1995. "The New Russian Regime" (in Russian). *Nezavisimaya Gazeta*, November 23, p. 5.

Gurr, Ted Robert. 1986. "The Political Origins of State Violence and Terror: A Theoretical Analysis." In Michael Stohl and George A. Lopez, eds., *Government Violence and Repression: An Agenda for Research.* Westport, CT: Greenwood, pp. 45–71.

Haggard, Stephan, and Robert Kaufman. 1996. *The Political Economy of Democratic Transitions.* Princeton, NJ: Princeton University Press.

———. 1997. "The Political Economy of Democratic Transitions." *Comparative Politics* 29(3): 263–283.

Hammer, Darrell. 1990. *The USSR: The Politics of Oligarchy.* 3rd ed. Boulder: Westview.

Handelman, Stephen. 1995. *Comrade Criminal: The New Russian Mafiya.* New Haven, CT: Yale University Press.

Hellman, Joel. 1998. "Winners Take All: The Politics of Partial Privatization." *World Politics* 50(2): 203–234.

Helmer, John. 1996. "Billions in War Funds Diverted." *Moscow Tribune.* April 1, p. 1.

Henderson, Conway. 1991. "Conditions Affecting the Use of Political Repression." *Journal of Conflict Resolution* 35(1): 120–42.

———. 1993. "Population Pressures and Political Repression." *Social Science Quarterly* 74(2): 322–333.

Hendley, Kathryn. 1997. "Legal Development in Post-Soviet Russia." *Post-Soviet Affairs* 13(3): 228–251.

Hoffman, David. 2002. *The Oligarchs: Wealth and Power in the New Russia.* New York: PublicAffairs.

Holland, Barbara, ed. 1985. *The Soviet Sisterhood: British Feminists on Women in Russia.* London: Fourth Estate.

Holmes, Stephen. 1997. "What Russia Teaches Us Now: How Weak States Threaten Freedom." *American Prospect* 33 (July–August): 30–39. Available online at http://epn.org/prospect/32/32holmfs.html. Accessed December 1, 1998.

———. 2001. "Simulations of Power in Putin's Russia." *Current History* 100(648): 321–328.

Holmgren, Beth. 1995. "Bug Inspectors and Beauty Queens: The Problems of Translating Feminism into Russian." *Genders* 22 (Fall): 15–31.

Holston, James, and Teresa P. R. Caldeira. 1998. "Democracy, Law, and Violence: Disjunctions of Brazilian Citizenship." In Felipe Agüero and Jeffrey Stark, eds., *Fault Lines of Democracy in Post-Transition Latin America.* Miami: North-South Center, pp. 263–288.

Hopkins, Mark. 1983. *Russia's Underground Press: The Chronicle of Current Events.* New York: Praeger.

Hosking, Geoffrey. 1992. *The First Socialist Society: A History of the Soviet*

Union from Within. 2nd enlarged ed. Cambridge: Harvard University Press.

Huber, Evelyne, Dietrich Rueshmeyer, and Joh D. Stephens. 1997. "The Paradoxes of Contemporary Democracy: Formal, Participatory, and Social Democracy." *Comparative Politics* 29(3): 323–342.

Human Rights Watch. 1991. "Prison Conditions in the Soviet Union: A Report of Facilities in Russia and Azerbaidzhan." Human Rights Watch/Helsinki. New York: Human Rights Watch.

———. 1992. "Hidden Victims: Women in Post-Communist Poland." Human Rights Watch/Helsinki. New York: Human Rights Watch.

———. 1995a. "Neither Jobs nor Justice: State Discrimination Against Women in Russia." Human Rights Watch/Helsinki. New York: Human Rights Watch/Women's Rights Project.

———. 1995b. "Crime or Simply Punishment? Racist Attacks by Moscow Law Enforcement." Human Rights Watch/Helsinki. New York: Human Rights Watch.

———. 1997a. "Russian Federation/Moscow: Open Season, Closed City." Human Rights Watch. New York: Human Rights Watch.

———. 1997b. "Russia/Too Little, Too Late: State Response to Violence Against Women." Human Rights Watch. New York: Human Rights Watch.

———. 1998a. *Abandoned to the State: Cruelty and Neglect in Russian Orphanages*. New York: Human Rights Watch.

———. 1998b. "Violence and Abuse Endemic in Brazil's Prison System." Human Rights Watch Electronic Report. December 15. Hrwatchnyc@igc.org.

———. 1998c. "Police Brutality Exacerbates Climate of Fear in Argentina." Human Rights Watch Electronic Report. Oct. 21. Hrwatchnyc@igc.org.

———. 1999. "The Russian Federation." *Human Rights Watch World Report 1999*. Available online at www.hrw.org/worldreport99/europe/russia.html. Accessed on June 15, 1999.

———. 2001. Russia/Chechnya: The "Dirty War" in Chechnya: Forced Disappearances, Torture, and Summary Executions 13 (1). New York.

Huntington, Samuel. 1991. "Democracy's Third Wave." *Journal of Democracy* 2(2): 12–34.

Huskey, Eugene. 1996. "Russian Judicial Reform After Communism." In *Reforming Justice*, pp. 325–347.

Hutton, Marcelline. 1996. "Women in Russian Society." In *Politics and Society*, pp. 63–76.

Ingram, Judith. 1999. "In Russia, Murder Rate Soars." Associated Press, April 30. From *Johnson's Russia List*, May 1, 1999.

Inkeles, Alex. "Introduction." In *On Measuring Democracy*, pp. i–x.

Isaenko, Anatoly V., and Peter W. Petschauer. 2000. "A Failure That Transformed Russia: The 1991–94 Democratic State-Building Experiment in Chechnya." *International Social Science Review* (Spring–Summer). Retrieved from Expanded Academic ASAP.

James, Barry. 1997. "Russia's Battered Women Find a Voice." *Irish Times On-line Edition*. March 15. Available at www.irish-times.com/irish-times/paper/1997/0315/hom16.html. Accessed on March 12, 1998.

Jancar-Webster, Barbara. 1978. *Women Under Communism*. Baltimore: Johns Hopkins University Press.

Javeline, Debra. 2003. *Protest and the Politics of Blame: The Russian Response to Unpaid Wages*. Ann Arbor: University of Michigan Press.

Jean, Francois. 2000. "Chechnya: Moscow's Revenge." *Harvard International Review* 22(3). Accessed from Infotrac OneFile.

Jelin, Elizabeth, and Eric Hershberg, eds. 1996. *Constructing Democracies*. Boulder: Westview.

Jhabvala, Farrakh. 1985. "The Soviet Bloc's View of the Implementation of Human Rights Accords." *Human Rights Quarterly* 7(4): 461–491.

Joseph, Richard. 1997. "Democratization in Africa After 1989: Comparative and Theoretical Perspectives." *Comparative Politics* 29(3): 363–382.

Juviler, Peter. 1977. "Women and Sex in Soviet Law." In *Women in Russia*, pp. 243–265.

———. 1998. *Freedom's Ordeal: The Struggle for Human Rights and Democracy in the Post-Soviet States*. Philadelphia: University of Pennsylvania Press.

Kagarlitsky, Boris. 1992. *The Disintegration of the Monolith*. London: Verso.

———. 1995. *Restoration in Russia: Why Capitalism Failed*. London: Verso.

———. 2003. "Kadyrov Won in Chechnya." *Moscow Times*, April 1. From *Johnson's Russia List*, April 1, 2003.

Kaiser, Robert. 1991. *Why Gorbachev Happened: His Triumphs and His Failure*. New York: Simon and Schuster.

Karatyncky, Adrian. 1999. "The 1998 Freedom House Survey." *Journal of Democracy* 10(1): 112–125.

Karl, Terry. 1990. "Dilemmas of Democratization in Latin America." *Comparative Politics* 23(1): 1–22.

———. 1997. "Democratization and Globalization: Reframing the Debate." Speech to the University of Costa Rica, San Jose, November 13.

Klimenkova, Tatiana. 1994. "What Does Our New Society Offer Russia?" In Anastasia Posadskaya, ed., *Women in Russia: A New Era in Russian Feminism*. Trans. Kate Clark. London: Verso, pp. 14–36.

Kolodko, Grzegorz W. 1998. "Russia Should Put Its People First." *New York Times*, July 7, p. A15.

Kotkin, Stephen. 2001. *Armageddon Averted: The Soviet Collapse, 1970–2000*. Oxford: Oxford University Press.

Kotz, David, with Fred Weir. 1997. *Revolution from Above: The Demise of the Soviet System*. London: Routledge.

Kovalev, Sergei. 1996a. "On the Observance of the Rights of Person and the Citizen in the Russian Federation 1994–95" (English version). Report of the President's Commission on Human Rights. Approved at the February 5, 1996, session of the commission.

———. 1996b. "On the New Russia." *New York Review of Books* 43(7): 10, 12.

Lapidus, Gail Warshofsky. 1977. "Sexual Equality in Soviet Policy: A Developmental Perspective." In *Women in Russia*, pp. 115–138.

————. 1978. *Women in Soviet Society: Equality, Development, and Social Change*. Berkeley: University of California Press.

Layard, Richard, and John Parker. 1996. *The Coming Russian Boom: A Guide to New Markets and Politics*. New York: The Free Press.

Leitzel, Jim. 1995. *Russian Economic Reform*. London: Routledge.

Leonard, Stephen T. 1997. "How 'Democratization' Came to Be: A Brief History of the Political Science of Change." Unpublished manuscript.

Lieven, Anatole. 1996. "Russia's Military Nadir: The Meaning of the Chechen Debacle." *National Interest* 44 (Summer): 24–33.

————. 1998a. *Chechnya: Tombstone of Russian Power*. New Haven, CT: Yale University Press.

————. 1998b. "History Is Not Bunk." *Prospect*. October. Available online at www.prospect-magazine.co.uk/highlights/lieven/index.html. Accessed on February 1, 1999.

————. 1999. "Russia Confronts Chechnya: Roots of a Separatist Conflict" (Review). *Europe-Asia Studies* 51(4): 720–722.

————. 2000. "Through a Distorted Lens: Chechnya and the Western Media." *Current History* 99(639): 321–328.

Linz, Juan, and Alfred Stepan. 1996. *Problems of Democratic Transitions and Consolidation: Southern Europe, Latin America, and Post-Communist Europe*. Baltimore: Johns Hopkins University Press.

Lipset, Seymour Martin. 1959. "Some Social Requisites of Democracy: Economic Development and Political Legitimacy." *American Political Science Review* 53(1): 69–105.

Los, Maria. 1988. *Communist Ideology, Law, and Crime: A Comparative View of the USSR and Poland*. London: MacMillan.

Lowenhardt, John. 1995. *The Reincarnation of Russia: Struggling with the Legacy of Communism, 1990–1994*. Durham: Duke University Press.

Madsen, Stig Toft. 1996. *State, Society, and Human Rights in South Asia*. New Delhi: Manohar.

Mauer, Marc. 1995. "The International Use of Incarceration." *Prison Journal* 75(1): 113–123.

————. 1997. "Americans Behind Bars: U.S. and International Use of Incarceration, 1995." Washington, D.C.: Sentencing Project.

McCormick, James M., and Neil J. Mitchell. 1997. "Human Rights Violations, Umbrella Concepts, and Empirical Analysis." *World Politics* 49(4): 510–525.

McFaul, Michael. 1997. "Democracy Unfolds in Russia." *Current History* 96(612): 319–325.

————. 2001. *Russia's Unfinished Revolution: Political Change from Gorbachev to Putin*. Ithaca, NY: Cornell University Press.

McNitt, Andrew D. "Some Thoughts on the Systematic Measurement of the Abuse of Human Rights." In *Human Rights Theory*, pp. 89–103.

Medvedev, Zhores. 1996. "Russia's Alcoholic Myth." *Moscow Times*, June 28, p. 10.

Mendelson, Sarah. 2002. "Russians Rights Imperiled: Has Anybody Noticed?" *International Security* 26(4): 39–69.

Menshchikov, Stanislav. 1990. *Catastrophe or Catharsis: The Soviet Economy Today*. Trans. Renfrey Clarke. London: Inter-Verso.

Merritt, Martha. 1997. "Review Essay: Contemplating Collapse and 'Democracy' in Russia." *Review of Politics* 59(2): 351–362.

Meyer, William. 1998. *Human Rights and International Political Economy in Third World Nations: Multinational Corporations, Foreign Aid, and Repression*. Westport, CT: Praeger Publishers.

Mironov, Oleg. 2002. "Report on the Activities of the Human Rights Plenipotentiary for the Russian Federation, 2001" (in Russian). Available online at www.ombudsman.gov.ru/docum/year-01.htm. Accessed on July 15, 2003.

Moscow Center for Prison Reform. 1993. *Prison Reform in the Former Totalitarian Countries: Issue 2*. Moscow: Moscow Center for Prison Reform.

———. 1996a. "Independent Submission: To the UN Human Rights Committee on the Periodic Report of the Russian Federation." Moscow: Moscow Center for Prison Reform.

———. 1996b. *In Search of a Solution: Crime, Criminal Policy, and Prison Facilities in the Former Soviet Union* (in Russian). Moscow: Prava Cheloveka.

Moscow Helsinki Group. 2000. *Human Rights in the Russian Regions*. Trans. Tanya Lokshina and MBS Services. Moscow: Zatsepa.

———. 2001. *Human Rights in the Russian Regions*. Trans. Tanya Lokshina, P. Razvin, and MBS Services. Moscow: Zatsepa.

———. 2003. "Situation of Prisoners in Contemporary Russia." Available online at www.mhg.ru/english/1E7AF09. Accessed September 10, 2003.

Moses, Joel. 1996. "The Communist Era and Women: Image and Reality." In *Politics and Society*, pp. 31–39.

Moynihan, Daniel. 1979. "The Politics of Human Rights." In *Human Rights Reader*, pp. 25–40.

Muller, Edward N. 1988. "Democracy, Economic Development, and Income Inequality." *American Sociological Review* 53(1): 50–68.

Nechemias, Carol. 1996. "Women's Participation: From Lenin to Gorbachev." In *Politics and Society*, pp. 15–30.

Nelson, Joan. 1994a. "How Market Reforms and Democratic Consolidation Affect Each Other." In Joan Nelson et al., *Intricate Links: Democratization and Market Reforms in Latin America and Eastern Europe*. Overseas Development Council, pp. 1–36.

———. 1994b. *A Precarious Balance: Democratization and Economic Reforms in Eastern Europe, Volume 1*. San Francisco: I.C.S.

Nemtsov, Alexander. 1995. "When People Drink, It's Society That Gets the Hangover." *Rossiiskiye Vesti*, December 2, pp. 12–13. In *Current Digest of the Post-Soviet Press* 47(49): 12–13.

Nivat, Anne. 2001. *Chienne de Guerre: A Woman Reporter Behind the Lines of the War in Chechnya*. Trans. Susan Darnton. New York: Public Affairs.

O'Donnell, Guillermo. 1993. "The Browning of Latin America." *New Perspectives Quarterly* 10(4): 50–53.

———. 1994. "Delegative Democracy." *Journal of Democracy* 5(1): 55–69.

———. 1996. "Illusions About Consolidation." *Journal of Democracy* 7(2): 34–51.

———. 1998. "Polyarchies and the (Un)rule of Law in Latin America." Working paper no. 254 for the Kellogg Institute for International Studies, University of Notre Dame.

O'Donnell, Guillermo, Philippe Schmitter, and Laurence Whitehead. 1986. *Transitions from Authoritarian Rule: Tentative Conclusions about Uncertain Democracies.* 4 vols. Baltimore: Johns Hopkins University Press.

"One Day in the Life of . . ." 1998. *Time International* 150(39), May 25. Accessed from Infotrac database.

Organization for Economic Cooperation and Development. 2001. Economic data for nonmember states. Available online at www.oecd.org/std/DNM/DataRUSQ.htm. Accessed on June 12, 2001.

Oxhorn, Philip. 1999. "When Democracy Isn't All that Democratic: Social Exclusion and the Limits of the Public Sphere in Latin America." Paper presented at the annual American Political Science Association Meeting, Atlanta, September 1999.

Park, Han S. 1987. "Correlates of Human Rights: Global Tendencies." *Human Rights Quarterly* 9(3): 405–413.

Partridge, Ben. 1998. "The East: Good Government Requires Better Prison Conditions." *Radio Free Europe/Radio Liberty Online Reports*, October 1. Available online at www.refrl.org/nca/features/1998/10/F.RU.9810011 31206.html. Accessed on June 10, 1999.

Paton-Walsh, Nick. 2003. "Russia Targets Sex Trade at Last." *The Guardian*, February 20. From *Johnson's Russia List*, February 20, 2003.

"Persecutions" (in Russian). 1996. *Express-Chronika*, May 31, p. 3.

Petro, Nikolai. 1995. *The Rebirth of Russian Democracy: An Interpretation of Political Culture.* Cambridge: Harvard University Press.

Pinheiro, Paolo S. 2000. "Democratic Governance, Violence, and the (Un)Rule of Law. Brazil Struggles with the Rule of Law as It Moves Toward Democracy." *Daedulus* 129(2). Accessed from Infotrac database.

Pipes, Richard. 1996. "Russia's Past, Russia's Future." *Commentary* 101(6): 30–38.

Plotnikov, Aleksandr. 1998. "After the Wedding." *Trud*, January 20, p. 7. In *Current Digest of the Post-Soviet Press* 50(3): 16.

Poe, Steven C., and C. Neils Tate. "Repression of Human Rights to Personal Integrity in the 1980s: A Global Analysis." *American Political Science Review* 88(4): 853–872.

Politkovskaya, Anna. 2001. *A Dirty War.* Trans. John Crowfoot. London: Harvill.

Posadskaya-Vanderbeck, Anastasia. 1998. "Redefining Democratization: The Gender Challenge." Available online at www.soros.org/wp/concept.htm. Accessed on October 1, 1998.

Powers, Nancy. 1999. "How Does Globalization Affect the Quality of Democratic Citizenship?" Paper presented at the annual meeting of the American Political Science Association, Atlanta, September.

Przeworski, Adam. 1986. "Some Problems in the Study of the Transition to Democracy." In Guillermo O'Donnell, Philippe C. Schmitter, and Laurence Whitehead, eds., *Transition to Democracy: Comparative Perspectives*. Baltimore: Johns Hopkins University Press, pp. 47–63.

———. 1991. *Democracy and the Market: Political and Economic Reforms in Eastern Europe and Latin America*. Cambridge: Cambridge University Press.

Quigley, John. 1989. "Human Rights Study in Soviet Academia." *Human Rights Quarterly* 11(3): 452–458.

Reanda, Laura. 1991. "Prostitution as a Human Rights Question: Problems and Prospects of United Nations Actions." *Human Rights Quarterly* 13(2): 202–228.

Reddaway, Peter. 1972. *Uncensored Russia: Protest and Dissent in the Soviet Union: The Unofficial Moscow Journal—A Chronicle of Current Events*. New York: American Heritage Press.

Reddaway, Peter, and Dmitri Glinski. 2001. *The Tragedy of Russia's Reforms: Market Bolshevism Against Democracy*. Washington, D.C.: United States Institute for Peace.

Reis, Fabio Wanderley. 1996. "The State, the Market, and Democratic Citizenship." In *Constructing Democracies*, pp. 121–137.

Reisinger, William, Andrei Melville, Arthur Miller, and Vicki Hesli. 1996. "Mass and Elite Political Outlooks in Post-Soviet Russia: How Congruent?" *Political Research Quarterly* 49(1): 77–101.

Remington, Thomas. 2002. *Politics in Russia*. 2nd ed. New York: Longman.

Remmer, Karen. 1991. "New Wine or Old Bottlenecks? The Study of Latin American Democracy." *Comparative Politics* 23(4): 479–495.

———. 1995. "New Theoretical Perspectives on Democratization." *Comparative Politics* 28(1): 103–122.

Remnick, David. 1997. "Can Russia Change?" *Foreign Affairs* 76(1): 35–49.

———. 1999. "Comment: More Bad News from the Gulag." *New Yorker* 74(46): 27–28.

Renfrew, Barry. 1999. "Russia Tries to Save Its Military." Associated Press. July 2. From *Johnson's Russia List*, July 3, 1999.

Reynolds, Maura. 2000. "War Has No Rules for Russian Forces Fighting in Chechnya." *Los Angeles Times*, September 17. From *Johnson's Russia List*, September 17, 2000.

Rodley, Nigel. 1994. "UN Rapporteur: Report on Russian Prisons" (in Russian). *Pravozashitnik* 1(3): 151–165.

Rodrik, Dani. 2002. "After Neo-liberalism, What?" November 19. Reprinted from the *Economic Times*. Available online at www.ksg.harvard.edu/news/opeds/2002/rodrik_neoliberalism_et_11902.htm. Accessed December 15, 2003.

Rueschemeyer, Dietrich, Evelyne Huber Stephens, and John Stephens. 1992. *Capitalist Development and Democracy*. Chicago: University of Chicago

Press.

Rule, Wilma. 1996. "Introduction: Equal Players or Back to the Kitchen." In *Politics and Society*, pp. 1–14.

"Russian Health Experts Present Latest 'Shocking Figures.'" 2001. *Obshchaya Gazeta*, March 1. From *Johnson's Russia List*, March 12, 2001.

Rustow, Dankwart. 1970. "Transitions to Democracy: Towards a Dynamic Model." *Comparative Politics* 2(3): 337–363.

Sabov, Aleksandr. 1998. "Femina." *Rossiiskaya Gazeta*, March 6, p. 9. In *Current Digest of the Post-Soviet Press* 50(10): 16–17.

Saivetz, Carol. 1996. "Russia: Problems and Prospects for Democratization." In *Establishing Democracies*, pp. 253–279.

Sakwa, Richard. 1994. *Russian Politics and Society*. London: Routledge.

Scheper-Hughes, Nancy. 1996. "Small Wars and Invisible Genocides." *Social Science and Medicine* 43(5): 889–900.

Schmitter, Philippe, and Terry Karl. 1991. "What Democracy Is . . . and Is Not." *Journal of Democracy* 2(3): 75–88.

Segal, Boris M. 1990. *The Drunken Society: Alcohol Abuse and Alcoholism in the Soviet Union—A Comparative Study*. New York: Hippocrene Books.

Semenoff, Lisa. 1997. "The Women's Movement and the Responses to Violence Against Women in the USSR and Post-Soviet Russia." Unpublished master's thesis, Carleton University, Ottawa, Canada.

Sergeev, Victor. 1998. *The Wild East: Crime and Lawlessness in Post-Communist Russia*. New York: M. E. Sharpe.

Serio, Joseph. 1992. *USSR Crime Statistics and Summaries: 1989–1990*. Translated from the Russian and edited by Joseph Serio. Chicago: Office of International Criminal Justice of the University of Illinois.

Shelley, Louise. 1987. "Inter-Personal Violence in the USSR." *Violence, Aggression, and Terrorism* 1(2): 41–67.

———. 1996. *Policing Soviet Society: The Evolution of State Control*. London: Routledge.

———. 2000. "Is the Russian State Coping with Organized Crime and Corruption?" In *Building the Russian State*, pp. 91–112.

———. 2003. "Crime and Corruption: Enduring Problems of Post-Soviet Development." *Demokratizatsiya* 11(1): 110–114.

Shenfield, Stephen. 1998. "On the Threshold of Disaster: The Socio-Economic Situation in Russia." Available online through the Federation of Independent Trade Unions website, www.trud.org/index 7–4.htm. Accessed on July 1, 1999.

Shtyleva, Lyubov. 1996. "Sexual Harassment on the Job." *Nezavisimaya Gazeta*, November 28, p. 6. In *Current Digest of the Post-Soviet Press* 48(50): 20.

Sieff, Martin. 2001. "Analysis: Putin's Costly Chechnya Victory." United Press International, April 2. From *Johnson's Russia List*, April 3, 2001.

Silverman, Bertram, and Murray Yanowitch. 1997. *New Rich, New Poor, New Russia: Winners and Losers on the Russian Road to Capitalism*. New York: M. E. Sharpe.

Smith, Gordon. 1991. *Soviet Politics: Struggling with Change*. 2nd ed. New York: St. Martin's.

"Sociological Analysis of Current Reforms." 1995. *Pravda*, March 15. From Foreign Broadcast Information Service (FBIS), SOV-95–066–5, pp. 79–85.

Solnick, Stephen. 2000. "Is the Center Too Weak or Too Strong in the Russian Federation?" In *Building the Russian State*, pp. 137–156.

Solomon, Peter. 1977. *Soviet Criminologists and Criminal Policy*. New York: Columbia University Press.

————. 1996. "The Bureaucratization of Criminal Justice Under Stalin." In *Reforming Justice*, pp. 228–255.

Solomon, Peter, and Todd Fogelsong. 2000. *Courts and Transition in Russia: The Challenge of Judicial Reform*. Boulder: Westview.

Solzhenitsyn, Alexander. 1974–1978. *The Gulag Archipelago: An Experiment in Literary Investigation*. Trans. by Thomas Whitney. New York: Harper and Row.

Sperling, Valerie. 1999. *Organizing Women in Contemporary Russia: Engendering Transition*. Cambridge: Cambridge University Press.

Stammers, Neil. 1995. "A Critique of Social Approaches to Human Rights." *Human Rights Quarterly* 17(3): 488–508.

Steele, Jonathan. 1994. *Eternal Russia: Yeltsin, Gorbachev, and the Mirage of Democracy*. Cambridge: Harvard University Press.

Stent, Angela, and Lilia Shevtsova. 1996. "Russia's Elections: No Turning Back." *Foreign Policy* 103 (Summer): 92–109.

Stetson, Dorothy McBride. 1996. "Law and Policy: Women's Human Rights in Russia." In *Politics and Society*, pp. 153–166.

Stiglitz, Joseph. 1999. "Whither Reform? Ten Years of the Transition." Keynote address to the annual World Bank Conference on Development Economics, April 30. From *Johnson's Russia List*, June 1, 1999.

Stites, Richard. 1978. *The Women's Liberation Movement in Russia: Feminism, Nihilism, and Bolshevism, 1860–1930*. Princeton, NJ: Princeton University Press.

Suny, Ronald G. 1998. *The Soviet Experiment: Russia, the USSR, and the Successor States*. Oxford: Oxford University Press.

Thomas, Dorothy, and Michele Beasley. 1993. "Domestic Violence as a Human Rights Issue." *Human Rights Quarterly* 15(1): 30–62.

UNICEF. 1997. "Children at Risk in Central and Eastern Europe: Perils and Promises," *Economies in Transition Studies*, Regional Monitoring Report, No. 4.

Uzelac, Anna. 2001. "Doing Time." *Transitions Online*, March 30, 2001.

Vaksberg, Arkady. 1991. *The Soviet Mafia*. Trans. John and Elizabeth Roberts. New York: St. Martin's.

Vandenburg, Martina. 2001. "We've Still Got a Long Way to Go." *Moscow Times*, March 7. From *Johnson's Russia List*, March 7, 2001.

Varoli, John. 1998. "Russia: Prison Reform Moves Forward, Slowly." September 3. *Radio Free Europe/Radio Liberty* electronic reports.

————. 1999. "Sexual Harassment, Russian Style." *St. Petersburg Times*, March 9. From *Johnson's Russia List*, March 11, 1999.

Waller, J. Michael. 1994. *Secret Empire: The KGB in Russia Today*. Boulder: Westview.

Walmsley, Roy. 1995. "Developments in the Prison Systems of Central and Eastern Europe." Paper no. 4 for the European Institute for Crime Prevention and Control. Helsinki: Heuni.

Waters, Elizabeth. 1991. "The Female Form in Soviet Political Iconography, 1917–32," In Barbara Evans Clements, Barbara Alpern Engel, and Christine D. Worobec, eds. *Russia's Women: Accommodation, Resistance, Transformation*. Berkeley: University of California Press.

Waters, T.R.W. 1996. "Crime in the Russian Military." London: Conflict Studies Research Centre.

Waylen, Georgina. 1994. "Women and Democratization: Conceptualizing Gender Relations in Transition Politics." *World Politics* 46(3): 327–354.

Weiler, Jonathan. 1999. "Human Rights in Post-Soviet Russia: Progress or Regression?" Unpublished diss. University of North Carolina–Chapel Hill.

———. 2002. "Human Rights in Post-Soviet Russia." *Demokratizatsiya* 10(2): 257–276.

Yavlinsky, Grigory. 2003. "Demodernization." Available online at www.eng.yabloko.ru. Accessed March 1, 2003.

Zakaria, Fareed. 1997. "The Rise of Illiberal Democracy." *Foreign Affairs* 76(6): 22–43.

———. 2003. *The Future of Freedom: Illiberal Democracy at Home and Abroad*. New York: W. W. Norton.

Zanger, Sabine C. 1998. "Dangerous Changes? The Effect of Political Regime Changes on Life Integrity Violations, 1977–1993." Paper presented at the Hinman Symposium on Democratization and Human Rights, Binghamton, New York, September 25–26.

Index

critic of economic reform, 101(n10); women's rights reporting, 77(n1)
Huskey, Eugene, 27(n36), 45–46, 96–97

ICCPR. *See* International Covenant on Civil and Political Rights
Illiberal democracies, 2, 22(n3), 27(n41)
Income inequality, 38–39, 127
"Intentional anarchy," 27(n36)
International Covenant on Civil and Political Rights (ICCPR), 57–58, 77(n4), 91
Isaenko, Anatoly, 107–108
Islam, 116
Ivanov, Igor, 90

Jean, Francois, 119(n11)
Jelin, Elizabeth, 57, 135(n5)
Judicial system: acquittal rate, 53(n49); in Brazil, 128; and corruption, 11, 45; decentralization of judicial authority, 43–45; inaccessibility of legal services, 51(n31); increase in caseloads, 44–45; jury trials, 47, 53(n49); lack of government spending on, 127; lack of horizontal accountability, 30, 45–46; pre-trial detention crisis, 30, 39–41, 44–45, 51(nn 31, 33), 52(n37); selective prosecution, 11; and sexual harassment, 79(n27); in Soviet era, 31–35. *See also* Prisons and prisoners
Juviler, Peter, 51(n33), 118(n4)

Kalinin, Yuri, 42, 52(n40)
Karl, Terry, 22(n1)
KGB, 30, 33
Kholodov, Dmitri, 96
Khrushchev, Nikita, 31
Kidnapping, 115–116, 120(n16)
Kolodko, Grzegorz, 135(n6)
Kotkin, Stephen, 12
Kotz, David, 10, 11, 24(n19)
Kovalev, Sergei: on Chechnya, 111, 117, 118(n4); human rights task force, 15; on poverty and nonpayment of wages, 23(n9); on prison conditions, 34–35; resignation from commission, 27(n37)
Kovalev Commission, 42, 43, 44, 52(n41)

Krasnador, race-based discrimination in, 94
Kulakov, Vladimir, 105(n45)
Kulikov, Anatoly, 37

Lapidus, Gail Warshofsky, 73
Latin America: decline in state spending, 134(n2); human rights violations following democratization and economic reform, 124–129, 135(n5); state violence, political opponents, and the poor, 23(n5)
Law enforcement: antiparasite laws, 49(n13); in Brazil, 128, 132, 135(n4); Decree 1226, 40, 94, 109; lack of government spending on, 11, 65–66; mafia–police complicity, 37; proliferation of microtyrannies due to lack of, 14; race-based discrimination, 91–95; in Soviet era, 31–35; violence toward women ignored, 56–57, 59, 63–64, 71–73. *See also* Prisons and prisoners
Lebed, Alexander, 112
Legal rights, defined, 4–5
Leitzel, Jim, 25(n21)
Lieven, Anatole: on anti-Russian commentators, 121(n24); on Chechnya, 111–112, 116, 118(n4), 119(n9), 120(n19); on corruption in government, 126; on military conscripts, 98–99; on teleological bias in research, 133
Life expectancy: decline in, 9, 25(n23); of women, 9, 62. *See also* Mortality rate
Life-integrity violations: defined, 3–4, 23(n8); in Latin America, 127–128, 132. *See also* Chechnya; Military conscripts; Murder; Orphans and orphanages; Prisons and prisoners; Race-based discrimination; Women
Linz, Juan, 27(n42)
Listyev, Vladimir, 37
Lokshina, Tanya, 53(n47)
Los, Maria, 40, 49(n13)
Luzhkov, Yuri, 91, 93–94, 103(nn 24, 25)

Mauer, Marc, 39
McCormick, James, 24(n12)
McFaul, Michael: on illiberal democra-

Police. *See* Law enforcement
Political prisoners, 33–34
Political rights: defined, 5; of women, 55, 64
Political Terror Scale (PTS), 3
Politkovskaya, Anna, 112, 115, 117, 120(n16)
Posadskaya-Vanderbeck, Anastasia, 70
Poverty: and increase in levels of crime and violence, 12, 30, 32; subsistence minimum, 79(n26). *See also* Economic reform
Press, freedom of, 27(n38)
Prisons and prisoners, 29–53; bail, 40, 51(n32); in Brazil, 128; decentralization of judicial authority, 43–45; Decree 1226, 40, 94, 109; harsh sentences for petty criminals, 37–38; improved conditions under Gorbachev, 33–34; increase in crime rate, 30, 34–37; and infectious disease, 42, 52(n40), 128; lack of accountability of prison authorities, 30, 45–46; lack of government spending on, 11, 30, 42–43, 52(n42), 53(n43); in late Stalin period, 48(n7); mass amnesty (2000), 51(n29); mass suicide, 52(n41); mortality rate, 47; nonpayment of wages for prison employees, 12; overcrowding, 39–40, 41–42, 51(n33), 52(n34), 128; physical abuse, 40–41, 52(n36); political prisoners, 33–34; pre-trial detention crisis, 30, 39–41, 44–45, 51(n31), 51(n33), 52(n37); race-based discrimination, 94; in Soviet bloc countries, 131–132; in Soviet era, 31–35; statistics (Soviet era), 32. *See also* Judicial system; Law enforcement
Privatization of state enterprises, 9–11; and corruption, 10–11, 126; in Poland, 135(n6); "spontaneous" privatization, 37
Prostitution: and economic upheaval, 12, 81(n43); international sex trade, 65, 74–76, 132; lack of attention paid to, 56
Psycho-neurological homes, 87
PTS. *See* Political Terror Scale
Putin, Vladimir: and Chechens, 93,

113–116, 118(n1), 121(n25); crackdowns on crime, 37–38; and decentralization, 14; and military, 97

Race-based discrimination, 89–95
Rape, 56, 70–73, 97
Reanda, Laura, 81(n43)
Reddaway, Peter: on budget deficit, 26(n29); on GDP, 9; on shock therapy, 10, 134(n1); on "value-subtracting" industries, 25(n21)
Red directors, 12, 126
Refugees: and Chechnya, 108, 114; and pre-trial detention crisis, 40; race-based discrimination, 89–95
Reynolds, Maura, 114
Riabtsev, Yevgenii, 71
Rodley, Nigel, 42
Rokhlin, Lev, 96–97
Romania, 131
Rule of law, 8, 132–133. *See also* Accountability, lack of; Crime; Judicial system; Law enforcement; Prisons and prisoners

Sabov, Aleksandr, 79(n22)
Sachs, Jeffrey, 10
Sakharov, Andrei, 33, 34
Samashki, 110–111, 119(nn 6, 7)
Scheper-Hughes, Nancy, 23(n6)
Segal, Boris, 73
Sergeev, Valery, 51(n28), 52(n37), 53(n43), 95
Sex trade. *See* Prostitution
Sexual harassment, 64, 68–70, 79(n27)
Sharapova, Olga, 101(n6)
Shelley, Louise, 33
Shenfield, Stephen, 6–7, 25(n21)
Shock therapy (economic reform), 7, 9–13, 24(n19), 74, 134(n1), 135(n6)
Shortages, 37, 50(n20)
Shtyleva, Lyubov, 69–70
Sieff, Martin, 119(n10)
Sinelnikov, Andrei, 80(n33)
SIZOs (pretrial detention centers), 39–42, 44–45, 51(n31), 51(n33), 52(n37)
Skinheads, 102(n17)
Slovakia, 131
Social and cultural rights, defined, 5
Social contract, 17–18
Social spending. *See* Fiscal austerity

About the Book

The connection between Soviet authoritarianism and human rights violations once seemed unassailable, as did the belief that a transition away from communist rule would lead to better protection of human rights. Challenging these assumptions, Jonathan Weiler contends that the tumultuous processes associated with political and economic reform have, in important instances, eroded human rights in post-Soviet Russia.

Weiler contends that, while Russia has moved rapidly toward a market-based economy, the social and legal elements of democratization have lagged behind. Examining the country's human rights record since 1991, he finds that the victims have changed—to the socially disadvantaged rather than the politically suspect—but the realities of life for the most vulnerable have in fact become worse. His work draws much-needed attention to this darker side of the post-Soviet transition.

Jonathan Weiler teaches Russian politics at the University of North Carolina at Chapel Hill.